Theological Reflection for Human Flourishing

Pastoral Practice and Public Theology

Helen Cameron
John Reader
Victoria Slater
with Christopher Rowland

scm press

© Helen Cameron, John Reader and Victoria Slater with
Christopher Rowland 2012

Published in 2012 by SCM Press
Editorial office
13–17 Long Lane,
London, EC1A 9PN, UK

SCM Press is an imprint of Hymns Ancient & Modern Ltd
(a registered charity)
13A Hellesdon Park Road
Norwich NR6 5DR, UK

www.scmpress.co.uk

British Library Cataloguing in Publication data
A catalogue record for this book is available
from the British Library

978-0-334-04390-4
Kindle 978-0-334-04463-5

Typeset by The Manila Typesetting Company
Printed and bound by
CPI Group (UK) Ltd, Croydon CR0 4YY

Contents

Acknowledgements

We thank the participants in the action learning event that took place at Ripon College Cuddesdon. We know that not all the experiences and discussion that took place are present in this book but we hope they will feel that we have captured the flavour of the occasion. We appreciate the risk they took in opening up a new conversation in the interests of human flourishing.

Tom Atfield, Stephen Belling, Stephen Blake, Mark Brennan, John Caperon, David Dadswell, Phillip Jones, Philip King, Jeff Leonardi, Anne Penn, Helen Peters, David Read, Robert Simmonds, Pam Wise, Roger Yates.

We also acknowledge with gratitude the administrative and research assistance of Phil Coull.

Introduction

This book tries to demonstrate that human flourishing is both a worthy topic for theological reflection and that theological reflection can contribute to the flourishing of those who practise it. This introduction outlines the two purposes of the book before describing how the book came to be written. It sets out the intended audience for the book and suggests ways of using the book. A brief introduction to the three main ideas in the title of the book is given by way of context for what follows, namely pastoral practice, public theology and human flourishing.

Purposes of the book

This book has two purposes. First, it seeks to provide an example of a process of theological reflection, offering a commentary on the practical problems encountered. Second, it seeks to bring into conversation two groups in the Church who have a shared concern about the impact of institutional structures on individuals but who rarely engage with each other directly.

The first purpose, that of providing a worked example of a process of theological reflection, seeks to answer a demand for examples to supplement the many excellent books of guidance on how to do theological reflection (Thompson and Pattison, 2005). Theological reflection is now taught to all those preparing for ministry and its practice is widely encouraged by most church traditions. The children's TV programme 'Blue Peter', is famous for giving children step-by-step instructions in a craft activity, but there comes a moment in the process when the presenter pulls the finished article from under the counter and says, 'Here's one I made earlier.' Part of learning a skill is to see what the end product might look like. However, this is not easily done with theological reflection. Part of our motivation for undertaking theological reflection is because it deals with an issue or context that matters to us. Reading about other peoples' issues may not sustain our interest as easily. Theological reflection is rarely a process without imperfections and so any attempt to share an example will also contain imperfections. This book contains a discussion of the successes and problems encountered in this example of theological reflection. Some readers may be heartened by the struggles of others, other readers may feel frustrated that what is presented is not a 'perfect' example.

The second purpose of the book is to trigger a conversation between two groups. The first group are those who while working in church-based pastoral ministry (often as priests or ministers) also engage with institutions outside the Church as a way of serving the communities in which they work. This institutional engagement may take the form of sitting on a school governing body, becoming a charity trustee, sitting on local partnerships and forums. Through these engagements they become aware of the complex structures that frame the lives of the individuals they encounter pastorally. The second group are chaplains and those Christians who work in institutions as professionals or managers (usually lay people). While the focus of their work is bounded by the institution that employs them, they are often engaged in pastoral care and so gain insights into the way in which structures affect individuals.

At first glance it might be assumed that these two groups would be in dialogue. However, church-based ministers often report feeling isolated in their institutional encounters, not knowing where to turn for advice or reflection on this un-expected aspect of their work. Chaplains, Christian profes-sionals and managers also report isolation in the issues they encounter in their work, feeling that the worshipping life of the local church does not touch on the pastoral dilemmas they wrestle with. Some of this isolation may be that when these groups meet in the local church the emphasis is on worship rather than reflection. It may also be that both sides feel in-hibited in engaging in theological reflection when they meet in contexts framed by secular institutions.

It is a key task of practical theology to identify the unheard voices and missing conversations in the life of the Church and make them audible. To use Paul's metaphor, there are some parts of the body that seem to have less prominence than others, yet all are vital to the functioning of the body (1 Corinthians 12). Practical theology seeks to direct attention to those things which the Church is overlooking but which can contribute to its part in God's mission to the world.

So to summarize. This book is about the process of theolog-ical reflection and offers a commentary on a specific example of a process of theological reflection. However, theological reflection has to be about something specific and in this book that something is the relationship between pastoral practice and public theology.

The conclusion that we came to as a result of undertaking this exercise in theological reflection is that both pastoral practice and public theology have a shared concern with hu-man flourishing and that the very process of engaging in theo-logical reflection can be an experience of human flourishing.

How the book came to be written

The idea for the book arose from a conversation between two theological research centres.

The William Temple Foundation has a long history of undertaking pioneering research in public theology. The Oxford Centre for Ecclesiology and Practical Theology is a newer research centre undertaking research into the practice of the Church in all its changing variety. Discussions between members of the two Centres led to a proposal to run an action learning event in which individuals from both groups described above could meet over 48 hours and try to do some shared theological reflection.

From the outset it was decided to use the pastoral cycle to shape the event as a straightforward method of theological reflection (see Chapter 1). However, it was recognized that there would be some particular challenges in using the method with a group of people who didn't know each other and who would only meet for this one event. First, the pastoral cycle assumes a shared context or issue, an assumption that couldn't be made for this event and so we needed a trigger that would help people decide if the event was for them, enable them to prepare an account of their experience before the event and then find points of connection when they met other participants. This trigger is described in Chapter 2. Second, the pastoral cycle assumes that the group will have a shared history of engaging with the Christian tradition. This was not the case and so we decided to enlist the help of Professor Christopher Rowland in helping the group understand the potential of engaging with scripture and identify themes from the Bible relevant to their discussion. This part of the process is described in Chapter 5. Third, the pastoral cycle aims to bring about transformation in the practice shared by the group members. In this case the aim of the event was to bring two groups into conversation in order to identify the things they had in common and the things they needed to hold in tension. The aim was that these 'solidarities and tensions' would be offered via this book to stimulate further conversation. This is recorded in Chapter 6.

The book has three authors with Chapter 5 having a response by Christopher Rowland. The authors are drawing on material from a wide range of participants. While the book has been edited to give a consistency of approach, there has been no attempt to 'iron out' the different voices contributing. Part of the reality of theological reflection is that it is a conversation between different voices and so listening in to an example of theological reflection requires tuning into the different voices taking part.

Intended audience

In line with the first purpose of this book, we hope that those seeking to learn about and practice theological reflection will find this book useful. It is likely that many such readers will be preparing for some form of authorized ministry in the Church. However, we hope that the book will also be an encouragement to those who facilitate theological reflection and find that there is sometimes a tension between the models on offer and what they are trying to do. We hope that the book will subvert any understanding of the pastoral cycle as a rigid linear tool but rather present it as a process that can deal with creativity and messiness.

Thinking of the second purpose of the book, we hope that the two groups that are brought into conversation (church-based ministers and institutionally-based chaplains, professionals and managers) will identify with this approach and seek to share it with their peers. The Conclusion will offer some specific encouragements to do this.

A final audience are students of pastoral, practical and public theology who are seeking to make connections between the different strands of the discipline of practical theology. The various institutional pressures on the discipline can lead to a separation of the strands, something which this book seeks to resist by proposing intellectual and practical connections. The authors share a conviction that the pastoral and political are connected and that it is often through examining practice that such connections become evident.

Ways of using the book

Chapter 1 sets out the understanding of theological reflection which informs this book. Chapters 2, 3, 4, 5, and 6 have a dual structure. Each has an opening and closing section which offers a commentary on how the process of theological reflection is worked out in the chapter. These sections 'bracket' the main substance of the reflection found in the chapter. The Conclusion, tries to draw together lessons both from the process of theological reflection and from the encounter between pastoral practice and public theology. For those reading the book with a primary interest in the challenges of doing theological reflection these sections may be worth special attention. Conversely, those more interested in the substantive issue the reflection is addressing may skim over those sections.

Chapters 3, 4 and 6 are subdivided into three sections dealing in turn with issues primarily affecting individuals, organizations and communities. The material in these chapters can be used as case studies when working with groups who do not share a context. Where groups do have a shared context it is preferable they work on shared material referring to the book as an example. These three chapters are longer than the rest. We would suggest that you read all the case studies in Chapter

4 and then in Chapters 5 and 7 just read the strand that interests you most. Otherwise be aware that there is a wide range
of material to absorb and sustain across the three chapters.

In addition to individual readers, we envisage the book
being read by groups of colleagues thinking of setting up a
theological reflection group as a way of exploring what some
of the challenges and rewards might be. We also envisage the
book being used as the basis for an in-service training event.

Setting the context – pastoral practice

Pastoral practice is used in this book to designate the care
provided by Christian professionals whether lay or ordained
and whether delivered in a church or secular context. It represents at least part of the work of all of the participants in
the event and many were also involved in the administration
and supervision of pastoral practice. It is evident from many
of the experiences they shared (see Chapter 3) that the context
within which they operate is changing.

Across the mainstream denominations there is a reduction
in the number of full-time paid ministers. Most ministers
either oversee several churches or work in a team with colleagues to cover a group of churches. This pattern of ministry
leads to regular reorganizations as the number of ministers
available or groupings of churches change. Flowing from this
is a greater expectation that lay people will be active in areas
formerly seen as the preserve of ordained ministers, such as
leading worship or pastoral care. This in turn is raising questions about what it means to minister and to whom the title
can rightly be applied (Heywood, 2011).

Alongside this there are new developments. New and ex-
perimental forms of worshipping community are emerging,
sometimes alongside existing congregations but sometimes

growing out of communities that are not connected with the Church but have a shared point of reference (Shier-Jones, 2009). There is also a growth in the number and range of ministries labelled chaplaincy done by a mix of lay and ordained people (Ballard, 2009). Again some are connected with existing churches but others are emerging in secular contexts such as shopping centres or sports clubs that seek a pastoral input.

John Reader (2008) has argued that the categories that are used in pastoral practice such as family, work and place have subtly changed in their meaning and that there is a danger of them being zombie categories where their content no longer matches reality. So for example, the Church may have an understanding of family in which women are available during the daytime to give time to the Church and where the whole nuclear family is available to take part in church activities on a weekly basis at evenings and weekends. A pattern of ministry based upon these assumptions will fail to connect with substantial numbers of families or will end up focusing exclusively on the limited number who do conform to this pattern. The Church can end up defining family life by who is available to fit into its pattern of activities rather than the pastoral needs of real families.

Much of the debate about the changes described above is framed in the language of mission. There is an emphasis on the essence of the Church being to contribute to the mission of God to the world. This is resulting in soul searching about how the Church should respond to its context (Cameron, 2010). The practical theologian Stephen Pattison (2008) has raised the concern that the intrinsic value of pastoral care is being lost to view. He argues that it is through the skilful attention to human need that the Church becomes aware of God at work in the world and so can decide how to respond. Much of the past scholarship on pastoral care aimed at uncovering its public and political dimensions. There is a danger that this is overlooked in focusing on missiology.

Changes within the secular context will be sketched in the final section on human flourishing.

Setting the context – public theology

Public theology is theology done in and about the public square. It is both the attempt to take part in public debates using Christian reasoning and also the task of thinking theologically about issues of public, social and economic policy. Elaine Graham (2008) argues that in the UK this type of theology has always been done in connection with pastoral and practical theology so that the political dimensions of caring for individuals and running institutions have been acknowledged and explored. This book tries to make the connections between those whose primary focus is the pastoral and those whose primary focus is policy as mediated through institutions. As such it stands firmly in this UK understanding of practical theology as a discipline that seeks to connect the personal and the political.

Within public theology there are think-tanks and institutes that aim to make a theological contribution to public debate. These would include organizations such as Theos, Ekklesia and the St Paul's Institute. There are others which are theologically informed but less overtly Christian in their work such as the Centre for Social Justice and ResPublica. Theos has argued consistently for a Christian secularism that seeks a plural public square where everyone can express their views without self-censoring their religious or other ethical beliefs.

The argument is that given the reality and increasing intensity of faith-based political differences, equal respect for

diverse citizens implies an acceptance of deliberative openness and a willingness to live with profound clashes of
moral conviction rather than trying to circumvent them in
pursuit of a premature consensus. (Chaplin, 2008, p. 56)

Within the Church and universities there are theologians
who focus on public theology or for whom it is an important
dimension in their work. The William Temple Foundation
brings together a number of Anglican theologians with this interest, such as Chris Baker, Elaine Graham, John Atherton and
John Reader. Their approach is explicitly inter-disciplinary.

This tradition does not attempt to colonize or convert public
life so much as establish a common space in which the language of value and ultimate meaning can be mediated across
confessional and institutional boundaries into a common
search for the stories we live by. (Graham, 2008, p. 16)

More recent work from this tradition tries to articulate guidelines that will offer 'a sense of direction for attaining greater
wellbeing for all' (Atherton, *et al.*, 2011, p. 121).

This teleological emphasis, in other words, describing what
a good society looks like, has a lot in common with Roman
Catholic approaches to public theology. The Catholic Bishops'
Conference of England and Wales put out a major statement
called *Choosing the Common Good*, prior to the 2010 general
election and in anticipation of the Pope's visit in the autumn
of 2010. It defines the good society as 'the sum total of social
conditions which allow people, either as groups or as individuals, to reach their fulfilment more fully and more easily'
(CBCEW, 2008, p. 8). It called for a restoration of social trust
in which each level of society more actively seeks the flourishing of the others and where people live in solidarity with each
other with a particular concern for the marginalized.

The Caritas Social Action Network followed up this work with three reports in 2011 articulating their response to the Government's Big Society Agenda. One of these reports was entirely devoted to theological and philosophical ideas that underpinned the Catholic response. This is an indication of the importance of official church teaching to the Roman Catholic approach to public theology and a desire to draw on that tradition in responding to particular political circumstances.

A further tradition drawing on the work of John Milbank and Stanley Hauerwas would see the Christian narrative as providing the most compelling vision of society. This would be evident in the work of theologians such as Luke Bretherton (2010). In this tradition there is greater suspicion of the Church being in partnership with the state in case the state co-opts the Church to its goals or turns the Church into an instrument of its policies. The primary responsibility of the Church is to witness to the Christ-event in the way it is organized and in what it does so that there is a clear alternative to a state and a market that fall short of the Christian vision. Another figure drawing on this approach is Philip Blond (2010) who has acknowledged John Milbank to be a key influence on his *Red Tory* agenda which he is now taking forward through his think-tank ResPublica.

This section has sought to sketch in a simplified way the context of public theology in the UK at present. For Christian practitioners interested in the political dimensions of their practice there is a growing range of resources to draw upon and a number of events and websites through which to join in the debate (see the Bibliography).

Setting the context – human flourishing

Since the advent of the Coalition government in May 2010, debates about human flourishing have become more lively and diverse. Their programme of major change in most areas of public policy, accompanied by cuts to public sector spending and a slowing down of economic growth have led to debates about what constitutes a good society.

This part of the chapter introduces some of those debates as a way of setting the scene for what follows.

The wellbeing debate

The debate about wellbeing is attractive for those who are interested in human flourishing. A desire to bring about life in all its fullness rather than bare survival involves participating in public debates that recognize that humans are more than economic animals with physical needs. The social policy academic, Hartley Dean offers a helpful exploration of the concept.

> There is a distinction to be made between being 'well enough' and being 'very well'. To be well enough is to be satisfied with what you have and do in life. To be very well is, perhaps to be 'truly fulfilled' as a human being. To be 'not well' implies some kind of deprivation. Significantly, of course, one cannot be 'excessively well' – this is a contradiction in terms. The notion of wellbeing is capable of invoking not just practical, but moral or ethical considerations about the extent and the limits of human need; not only a 'thin' conception of what the lives of human beings necessarily entail, but also a 'thick' conception of what a human life ought to or potentially could entail. (Dean, 2010, p. 100)

The Office of National Statistics led a major national debate in Spring 2011 about what factors are important for wellbeing. The things that came out as most important to people were: health, living in a good environment, relationships (family, work, community including faith community), work–life balance, availability of green space, opportunities for creativity and self-expression. There was a consistent theme that a good society was a fair society. The Office of National Statistics have proposed a set of objective and subjective measures to capture these aspects of wellbeing and will start to publish data on the wellbeing of the UK population in 2012. This will enable the wellbeing of people in different places and with different characteristics to be compared. It offers Christian practitioners the opportunity to comment on the wellbeing of those they serve and the particular dimensions of wellbeing they seek to support.

It seems as if each government tries to develop its own understanding of poverty. The New Labour government focused on social exclusion and the barriers to participating in what the rest of the population would regard as the normal activities of life. The Coalition government have picked up those themes, but by using wellbeing as a measure set alongside economic progress, they are emphasizing the role that family and community play rather than just the role of government.

Alison Webster (2002) in her theological commentary on wellbeing suggests that the distinctive thing that Christian spirituality has to offer is structures of meaning for the bad things that happen in life so that they too may be incorporated into a personal quest for wellbeing.

> The temptation to explain away sickness death and loss is ever present, particularly for religious people. It is important, in the face of traumatic life experiences, to hold on to the value of mystery. Crass explanations can undermine human wellbeing, while embracing mystery can enhance it. (Webster, 2002, p. 144)

The Big Society debate

The Big Society was an important if poorly understood plank of the Conservative Party manifesto in the 2010 election. It was seen as a firm response to the persistent suggestion that the Conservative Party does not 'believe in society'. The Coalition adopted it as policy and its substance has gradually emerged. There are three main strands: social action, public service reform, and community empowerment. It is intended that this will work at personal, community and state level. Individuals are being encouraged to give more time and money to philanthropic causes. Communities are being given the opportunity to contest the way in which public services are provided and then bid to deliver those services themselves. At government level, public sector reform involves breaking down large providers into smaller units either managed by those who work for them or by community stakeholders. Initiatives falling under the Big Society policy banner include:

- Training community organizers to mobilize communities for action.
- Giving young people the opportunity to experience the National Citizen Service.
- Devolving more decision-making powers to local authorities while at the same time giving community groups the right to challenge those decisions. This involves making more information about government spending and assets available to the public.
- Diversifying the range of organizations that provide public services such as co-operatives and social enterprises.
- Using dormant bank accounts to fund community groups.

This complex and growing set of proposals are signalling a significant shift in responsibility between the different sectors of society. The household is being given first place, followed by the community but there is also a commitment to increase the role of the private sector as a guarantor of choice and quality. The debate is whether all households are equally able to take more responsibility for the welfare of their members and whether citizens in all communities are able to form grassroots organizations to deliver services which might once have been the remit of the state. As a result, some commentators have argued, we will not have a Big Society, but many differently served societies.

Despite these reservations, churches have on the whole responded positively to this policy emphasis. The Church of England has received funding to develop inter-faith relations in five areas. The Roman Catholic Church has emphasized its existing philanthropic work and its capacity to respond further to new opportunities. The Methodist Church debated the issue at its 2011 Conference and resolved to look again at the way its resources are deployed. The social action of the local church has been given a new significance as an exemplar of the community action the government seeks. All this has led to greater debate within and between the churches about the vision of society they wish to promote.

The debate about localism and early intervention

The New Labour Government placed great emphasis on a combination of tax and benefits to move families with children out of poverty. They also stressed the importance of development in early childhood by opening Children's Centres which brought together the services that support those with pre-school children. The critique offered by the Coalition government was that this had not been enough and that cash transfers alone do not move a family out of poverty.

New Labour also invested heavily in regeneration, in particular the physical regeneration of housing, public buildings (such as schools) and green spaces. The appearance of many deprived communities was transformed. However, there were many post-industrial communities (former mining, steel and fishing towns) that did not regain an economic rationale. It was recognized that social and economic regeneration present a greater challenge and towards the end of their term in office experiments were occurring to merge different public sector budgets to deliver agreed community ends.

The Coalition has retained the emphasis on child poverty but with a reduced emphasis on benefits and tax transfers and a strong endorsement of early intervention. The responsibility to deliver on early intervention lies with local authorities most of whom are struggling to deal with statutory responsibilities in the face of budget cuts. There is also an emphasis on place but delivered through putting more responsibility into the hands of local citizens to set up institutions such as free schools, social enterprises and mutuals that can bid to run public services.

Ultimately there is no policy choice between investing in people and investing in place. People both shape and are shaped by the place in which they live. As this book will show, a key dilemma for Christians working in marginalized communities is to know whether to focus their efforts on individuals or on the structures which shape their lives.

The debate about procurement and personalization

In a resource-constrained environment attention is drawn to taxes that are not well spent. Better value is seen to come from procuring goods and services in greater bulk to allow for economies of scale and to save time specifying requirements. However, there is an enduring desire to deliver choice in public services in the belief that this feeds back into service-providing organizations, making them more competitive and responsive. This means that the personalization of budgets for individuals in receipt of care is still seen as a priority.

A danger of personalization is that the transaction costs and responsibilities of wrong choices tend to rest with the service recipient who is not able to pool their risk with others in the same situation. A danger of large-scale procurement is that the needs of specific contexts are ignored and that service-provision is treated as a commodity rather than something that is only as good as the relationship between service giver and service user. This set of dilemmas links to the Catholic concept of subsidiarity which includes a desire that services should be provided at the most appropriate level in society but with each level having a responsibility for the effectiveness of the others.

This section of the chapter has sought to set the political context for the debate on human flourishing. The next chapter introduces the approach to theological reflection used in this book.

I

How can Theological Reflection be Used?

Why do theological reflection?

One of the core tensions that Christian people have always had to engage with is the daily challenge of how to live faithfully in the context in which they find themselves. In the contemporary cultural context of a fluid, plural, postmodern and post-Christendom society characteristic of Western culture, this is no easy matter. One response to the challenges that this poses could be to withdraw into the carapace of religious identity, seeking to remain separate and secure from the ever-shifting complexity of contemporary cultural life. This is the way of separation. Holding on to one's own cherished beliefs and ways of seeing the world may be comforting but represents a lack of engagement with the world that inevitably leads to the atrophy of faith rather than to the growth, renewal and transformation that comes from the willingness to engage in genuine dialogue with the world that God creates and loves. If one begins with a theology of Creation that understands God to be present at the heart of Creation, actively engaged in drawing the whole of Creation into wholeness in Christ, it follows that if we are to live faithfully then we need to pay attention to the world; to listen to what God might be saying through our encounters within it; to be open to learn from our encounters and, by implication, to be willing to change in response to what we learn. This is the way of encounter, characterized by the humility of being willing to engage in genuine dialogue.

It is within the kind of approach characterized here as the way of encounter that theological reflection takes its place. At a basic level, one is confronted with the question: how can I discern how to act faithfully in the world if I do not reflect on both my faith and my experience of the world? When looked at in this way, theological reflection can be said to be fundamental to living faithfully in the world: it is the process through which we constantly deepen our understanding of ourselves, others and God and of how we integrate this understanding in our lives so that what we do becomes congruent in any given context with who we are as people and as communities of faith. In this view, theological reflection is not something that theologians do, nor is it merely an intellectual exercise; rather theological reflection lies at the heart of the Christian commitment to live faithfully in the world for the sake of the world that God loves. It is itself 'a process of coming to know God through reflecting on God's world in the light of resources from the tradition' (Thompson, 2008, p. 57).

Approaches to theological reflection

Many different approaches to theological reflection have been taken and several different models have been developed. A useful basic summary of some of these can be found in the *SCM Studyguide to Theological Reflection* (Thompson, 2008). All the models involve in some way bringing into awareness and dialogue three contexts: the context of the reflector with their beliefs, values, spirituality, personal experience and world view; the contemporary context which the reflector encounters; the context and resources of the faith tradition. The process enacts what is at best a mutually nourishing conversation that may issue in new theological and practical insights and the possibility of transformative action. Most of the models have been developed from an approach to learning from experience referred to as the pastoral cycle. This provides the basis for a theoretical understanding of the process of reflection on pastoral practice and is the basis of the approach taken in this book. This chapter will introduce the pastoral cycle as a basic model of learning for the development of new insight and practice before discussing its relevance in relation to the concept of 'blurred encounters' discussed more fully in Chapter 2.

Learning through reflection on practice

The pastoral cycle developed out of a growing awareness in secular professions in the second half of the twentieth century of the importance of reflection on practice as a source of learning; reflective practice became an accepted component of professional training particularly in the fields of education and nursing. In 1983 Donald Schon wrote *The Reflective Practitioner: How Professionals Think in Action*, and in 1984 Donald Kolb formulated the process as an 'experiential learning cycle'.

In this model there are four stages in the cycle of learning:

1. Identification of a specific experience.
2. Reflecting on the experience at one remove as an observer rather than an actor.
3. Deriving and applying general rules, principles or concepts from the experience.
4. Trying out new ways of acting in the light of new insights and choices that emerge.

Like all models, this over-simplifies how things happen in life and is unable to represent the complexities of human interactions and relationships, but what it does do is draw attention to the value of consciously standing back from the situation

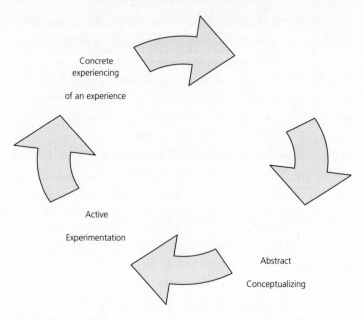

Concrete
experiencing

of an experience

Active

Experimentation

Abstract

Conceptualizing

that we are in so that we can reflect on and learn from it, thus deepening our insight and enabling us to develop practice. Thompson points out (Thompson *et al.*, 2008, p. 21) that at their simplest, all such cycles have three phases:

SEE – REFLECT – ACT

In order to relate to a specific discipline this may be expanded into:

*EXPERIENCE – REFLECTION –
THEORY – ACTION*

As many writers have noted, the process may be represented more appropriately as an open-ended spiral rather than a closed circle, as once the cycle has resulted in newly informed action, the cycle of reflection begins again.

The pastoral cycle

It is this basic experiential learning cycle that has been developed into the pastoral cycle. The key difference to Kolb's cycle is the incorporation of theological insight from the faith tradition of the reflector. The central assumption to note in this approach is that theory and practice are not separate but inextricably joined. As Graham, Walton and Ward state in *Theological Reflection: Methods*, 'practice is both the origin and the end of theological reflection, and 'talk about God' cannot take place independent of a commitment to a struggle for human emancipation' (Graham, Walton and Ward, 2005, p. 170). Although there are many variations of the pastoral cycle, the basic hermeneutic process involves:

Identification of a specific experience/situation
↓
*Building a multi-layered description from as many
perspectives as possible including one's own
This is sometimes called a 'thick' description*
↓
*Critical reflection drawing on appropriate perspectives,
for example historical, sociological, psychological,
economic, theological*
↓
Engaging in dialogue with the appropriate faith tradition
↓
*Allowing time and space for new insight and
understanding to emerge*
↓
*Deciding on and planning action in the light of what
has emerged*
↓

5

Implementing the course of action
↓
Begin another cycle of reflection...
↓

The main elements of the pastoral cycle process can therefore be identified as:

Identification of an issue or situation that needs to be reviewed

The hermeneutic process begins with a group or individual agreeing that a specific issue, situation or practice needs to be examined in order to gain fuller understanding of what is being done and why.

Building a 'thick' description

Time is then spent describing and analysing the situation as fully as possible. As many factors as possible that relate to the situation are explored and a multi-layered description is built up in order to gain as comprehensive an understanding of the situation as possible.

Engaging in critical reflection

Reflectors then take time to think through the elements that have emerged. Insights and observations are shared and the process can draw upon resources from scripture and tradition as well as from other relevant disciplines. Critical questions are asked of the subject of reflection; prayer, silence, play, and creativity may play their part in illuminating the subject and revealing insight. Staying with doubt, confusion and not knowing may also be part of this process, trusting that insight and understanding may eventually be revealed.

Making decisions and planning

If the reflection has been well thought through, it will usually issue in the recognition of decisions that need to be made. Decisions need to be owned by those involved or they will not be implemented. A good facilitator will ensure that a consensus or a majority decision is reached in a way that allows everyone to feel part of the process and everyone's voice to be heard.

Implementing the action plan

Ensuring that the agreed decisions are acted upon may be one of the more difficult parts of the process. In order to achieve implementation, it is helpful to be specific about what needs to happen, who is responsible for each aspect of the process, when things need to happen and how progress will be reviewed.

Continuing the cycle

Any change that occurs as a result of this process presents a new context and therefore new material for reflection.

What's the use of theological reflection?

The problem with all process models of experience is that they can be misunderstood as representing a rational, sequential and invariable patterning of reality, whereas models only ever represent an ideal representation of elements of the real process.

In reality, insights, understandings and the different elements of the process may happen at different times and in different ways. As this book attests, the process will usually be much more complex and messier than the model implies. However, this does not detract from the value of keeping a model of the process of reflection in mind.

When people are asked whether or not they set aside designated time to reflect on practice, it is not uncommon to hear the response, 'Oh well, I do that all the time.' It is important to be clear that ruminating on work is not the same as engaging in intentional theological reflection. The value of having a model to guide reflection has many aspects:

- It enables us to become conscious of what we are doing.
- It challenges us to make time to do it, to make time to attend and to listen.
- It invites us to make the effort to utilize different resources that may be available.
- It provides a framework for reflecting with others in order to expand our experience and perspectives and to open ourselves to new challenges.
- It provides a framework for articulating what we are doing to ourselves and to others.
- It helps us to choose an intentional way of working that is open to creative change, development and transformation.
- It provides a discipline of practice.

This approach suggests that in order to remain faithful practitioners in the world we need to continually review what we are doing, why we are doing it and whether we are doing it in the most appropriate, effective and creative way. On a deeper level, theological reflection challenges us to attend and listen to ourselves, our context, the tradition and God in the hope and expectation that the Holy Spirit will continually reveal new things if we dare to look and have eyes to see and hearts to respond.

Intentional theological reflection is not only important in relation to what we *do* as people of faith in the world: doing and being are inextricably bound together and theological reflection relates equally to a deepening understanding of who we are as people of faith and to how that understanding and identity flows out into transformative action and presence in the world. At this level, taking time to consciously reflect on our experience of the world in the light of the resources of the Christian tradition is a discipline that can help us to:

- gain a fuller understanding and a deepening of the meaning of discipleship
- develop new insight, creativity and depth of understanding in our pilgrimage of faith
- integrate our faith with the whole of our lives
- gain a deeper awareness of ourselves as people of faith.

Prayer, our relationship with God and our capacity to wait on God in order to discern what God wishes to reveal to us through a given situation lie at the heart of theological reflection. In this sense, it can be seen as a contemplative practice in which, at best, the whole of our being is involved: it is a graced process that can help us to see more clearly how we might participate in God's unfolding purpose for the world.

An example of theological reflection in the Christian tradition

Within the Christian tradition, the process of theological reflection can be illustrated with reference to the description of the walk to Emmaus in Luke's Gospel (Luke 24.13–35). As two of the disciples walk together to Emmaus, they reflect in conversation on the events that they have witnessed and been part of in Jerusalem. As they reflect on the trial and crucifixion of Jesus and all that has happened, 'Jesus himself drew near and went with them' but they could not recognize him; he seems a stranger. When Jesus asks them about their conversation they relate to him the events that have taken place and speak of the hope that they had held that 'he was the one to redeem Israel', hope which now seems to have been demolished. Luke tells us that they looked sad, their disappointment and grief betrayed in their countenance. In response, Jesus draws into the conversation the resources of the faith tradition, 'And beginning with Moses and all the prophets, he interpreted to them in all the scriptures the things concerning himself.' The three partners in conversation continue on to the village, the two disciples no doubt still reflecting on the situation that they cannot understand and on their encounter with this stranger who has opened the scriptures to them in relation to it. They carry on, disappointed and sad, perhaps still wondering, really, what it all might mean. However, something prompts them to stay with this encounter, to beg the stranger to stay with them. And as they sit down together at table to eat, Jesus 'took the bread and blessed, and broke it, and gave it to them.' Through that by now familiar gesture, they recognize that Jesus is indeed with them and that the story of the empty tomb and the resurrection that the women in Jerusalem had proclaimed no longer seems to them 'an idle tale' (Luke 24.11). Everything is transformed in the light of this revelation as they return to Jerusalem to continue their reflection on their experience and the faithful practice of their lives both as individuals and as a community in the light of their illuminated experience and transformed understanding.

Theological reflection and blurred encounters

The key elements of the process of theological reflection can easily be drawn out from the story of the walk to Emmaus. It begins with an initial encounter between the followers of Jesus with their own identity and understanding of experience and, in this case, the brutal and disorientating events in their contemporary world. They do not know how to make sense of the events they have encountered and so instinctively they start the process of reflecting together on what has taken place. This bruising encounter with death, loss and the fragmentation of meaning takes them to a strange and unfamiliar place, a place where many of the certainties and assumptions of their life together with Jesus no longer seem to hold. They are thrust into a place of not knowing, a liminal space where many of the old certainties have disappeared and they do not know what that means for their lives. It is indeed apt that they are on a journey, in between one known place and the next, a resonant location for liminal experience. It is a deeply challenging place to be. It poses to them questions of meaning and identity: What does this experience mean? What does it say to us? Who are we, followers of Jesus, now that Jesus is gone? How should we respond in these particular circumstances? What help is to be found in this unfamiliar place?

It is precisely this trajectory that can be described in the context of 'blurred encounters'. In *Entering the New Theological Space,* Reader and Baker describe this as a dialogic journey from 'encounter' to 'purposive threshold', the liminal space that can be revelatory of new insight (Reader and Baker, 2009, p. 220). These encounters occur when people of faith find themselves engaged with events and experiences in and of the contemporary world which lead into strange and liminal spaces that can be disorientating and may even feel disempowering. The question to be asked is: how can we negotiate being in unfamiliar or liminal places such that the experience is not ultimately one of powerlessness and meaninglessness but one that becomes a creative place that may yield new insight and may be transformative of practice? Many Christians find themselves in such situations in the contemporary world and the following chapters describe a series of such encounters. As you read these chapters it will become clear that the examples given raise fundamental questions about how people of faith engage with situations in the contemporary world.

These include questions such as:

- What qualities do we need to bring to such encounters if they are to be creative?
- What helps us to discern how to respond?
- What part does theological reflection play in helping people of faith in their encounters with the complexities of our contemporary world?

In other words, as we move from initial encounters into threshold or liminal spaces that are unfamiliar and often disorientating, how do we both remain faithful and at the same time be open and responsive to the potential for the revelation of new insight and understanding that the encounter may unfold? In *Entering the New Theological Space*, Reader and Baker identify certain principles and virtues that may enable fruitful dialogue in this kind of context. A central principle is to be willing to enter the encounter with an attitude of openness, a willingness to risk entering into genuine dialogue with others across boundaries, for example, of faith, denomination or culture. This implies a willingness to risk negotiating one's identity in response to the encounter. The two virtues that Reader and Baker identify are authenticity and faithfulness. The quality of authenticity derives from knowing the values that one brings into a strange situation and having confidence in one's core identity. The quality of faithfulness derives from acknowledging the faith traditions and institutions that have nourished us along with the resources both spiritual and material that they provide and from remaining faithful to our understanding of Christian identity, an understanding often expressed in the quality of solidarity with and commitment to the people and situations that we encounter, even the most difficult ones. Such basic principles and virtues can help us to enter 'blurred encounters' with courage and optimism, allowing us to see them as places of potential insight, creativity, transformation and witness rather than places of difficult challenge against which we would prefer to defend ourselves from within rigid and inflexible identities.

This theological method of dialogic engagement with the contemporary world characterized by openness to emergent insight takes us back to the beginning of the chapter and the basic question of how to engage faithfully with the contemporary world. If one embarks upon the way of encounter then the importance of theological reflection within this approach becomes evident. It is certainly a skill that requires commitment and practice, but more than this, it is a way of developing a faithful orientation towards the whole world because, ultimately, it is about consciously orientating oneself towards God. As suggested earlier, in this sense, it is a contemplative practice, a way of seeing reality that develops our capacity to be open to and faithful in every situation. In an unpublished paper titled 'Is Theological Reflection a Technique or a Virtue?', John Swinton suggests that theological reflection cannot be understood apart from the development of a type of contemplative character, 'then theological reflection might be best understood as a virtue which contributes to the development of Christian character which in turn enables approaches to exploring the Christian tradition which are faithful and transformative both to the theologian and to the particular situations and experiences she is examining' (Swinton, 2009).

This chapter has given a brief indication of one strand of the development of theological reflection from Kolb's experiential cycle of learning, through the pastoral cycle model and into a discussion of how this relates to the context of 'blurred encounters'. We have ended with the suggestion that theological reflection in such complex, challenging and highly fluid contexts can be seen most helpfully as a virtue which, if practised faithfully, may become a *habitus*, a way of being and seeing in the world which helps to establish our character as Christians, continuously orientated towards God. Whatever our life context, every Christian person will at times, willingly or unwillingly, find themselves encountering situations and experiences in which it is not easy to know how to respond faithfully. The dialogical process of theological reflection, if it becomes a habit, can be a valuable resource for enabling us to be open to such situations and so to the Christ who walks with us in every encounter, strange and unfamiliar though it may be, ready to reveal new insight for the sake of the world, if we have eyes to see.

'"Did not our hearts burn within us while he talked to us on the road, while he opened to us the scriptures?" And they rose that same hour and returned to Jerusalem' (Luke 24.32–3). The disciples entered into and stayed with the place of not knowing, of confusion and doubt, of pain and perplexity, where certainty and answers ran out. In their desire to see and to understand what meaning it could hold they were willing to remain open to the stranger they encountered and to listen to the faith tradition that he interpreted to them. In the end, in the most familiar gesture of the breaking, blessing and sharing of the bread, they saw that Jesus was with them. This revelation of insight and new understanding illuminated the meaning of the events that a moment before had so perplexed them and they returned to Jerusalem ready for transformed action and presence in the world. And, of course, as the New Testament attests, the process of theological reflection continued.

2

Triggering the Conversation: Introducing Blurred Encounters

Introductory commentary

The first question we were faced with in planning the action learning event was: what will trigger participants' desire to pay for and attend an event that engages them in theological reflection? In our experience of seeing theological reflection used in pastoral practice, it is often a non-routine decision such as changes to the Church's buildings or leadership structures that would generate the energy to engage in theological reflection. Such situations in the local church involve participants who know each other well and have a shared interest in the wellbeing of the church community and a shared experience of engaging with the Christian tradition. None of these three things would apply in bringing together people who we felt should be in conversation with each other but who didn't know each other and who would be coming together for a one-off event. We needed a trigger that would provoke recognition and commitment from our invited participants.

We quickly arrived at an idea that had caught our imaginations, that of 'blurred encounters'. This was an idea that John Reader had developed from his ministry of constantly crossing and re-crossing the boundary between pastoral practice and institutional engagements. In this chapter, John sets out that idea. The idea had personal resonances for the other two authors as well. Victoria Slater has spent all her ministry in various forms of chaplaincy and is currently doing research into new forms of chaplaincy that are emerging and how the Church is responding to them. She identified with the concept of blurred encounters from her ministry and felt other chaplains would do so. Helen Cameron brought her experience of offering consultancy to the life of the Church and the sense that there was a release in acknowledging the messiness of practice.

These autobiographical resonances are not surprising. Our hunches come from somewhere and the connections we make with people and ideas come from moments of recognition. We would see these disclosures as being part of the way in which practical theology moves forward. The intellectual capacity to reason that we bring, needs to be partnered with openness to something that we recognize but can only rationalize in retrospect.

The invitation to the event gave a short description of blurred encounters and invited participants to submit an example from their own practice which could be circulated to other participants beforehand. We were excited when we had acceptances from people who represented the two groups we had in mind and when the examples they produced chimed with our understanding of blurred encounters.

A definition of blurred encounters

A blurred encounter is a pastoral situation in which boundaries are likely to be crossed and where the Christian will need to make a judgement as to the appropriate course of action. This implies the presence of other complications. These might include: the possibility of a compromise of one's faith position;

the need to cross a boundary of some sort, geographical, cultural or ideological; the taking of risks in order to respond creatively; the knowledge that some people may be opposed to or offended by the decision taken. To use contemporary language, the minister or practitioner will find themselves 'outside their comfort zone' and out in unknown or unfamiliar territory where previous rules and conventions do not easily apply.

Why and where do such situations occur? They occur whenever one finds oneself outside the confines of one's faith group, and they happen increasingly because significant numbers of people do not share, in this case, a Christian commitment. So we are not simply talking about the experiences of ministers encountering those of other faiths or none, but of lay Christians attempting to live out their faith in workplace, leisure and family settings.

Another useful way of thinking about this is by using the analogy of eating or being eaten. When encountering the challenge of crossing a boundary or of compromising a belief, the alternative is either to remain firmly on one side and refusing to budge – in which case the risk is that the person of faith 'eats' or 'consumes' the other – or of moving too far across to the other side, in which case the risk is of being 'eaten' or appropriated by the other. This image comes from the work of the French philosopher Derrida and seems a particularly powerful way of describing the feelings we often have when meeting this challenge (Reader, 2005, p. 8). The reality is that, in a genuine encounter, where both sides take the risk of being changed and re-thinking their position, it is impossible to avoid 'being eaten'. So the best thing to work towards is 'being eaten well', where change does take place but not at the cost of integrity or of abandoning core beliefs. Hence blurring is inevitable in genuine encounters between Christian practitioners and the world.

Blurred encounters in parish life

Here is an example from parish ministry. Most ministers are faced with the prospect of conducting occasional offices – funerals, weddings and baptisms – where the family are intent on personalizing the service in some way. It is common to receive requests for favourite pieces of secular music, for instance, to be played during the ceremony, often on CD or I-Player. Where does one draw the line and on what grounds? The more this happens, and the more that non-church couples experience this at the services of their friends, the more it becomes the norm and the harder it becomes to resist, if one should choose to do so. Knowledge of traditional hymns is now extremely limited, often to what one of the couple has sung at school or else the Rugby Union repertoire in some parts of the country. What they have seen on TV becomes another model of what they want and expect. A couple recently bought in a black gospel choir for their wedding and built the service around their performances of 1960s and 1970s soul music, with the addition of one hymn. Was the minister concerned right to agree to this? He was thanked afterwards and told that this was not just a wedding but a 'happening'! While not sure that he was comfortable presiding at 'happenings', he did believe that the pastoral contact created might yet 'bear fruit'.

No doubt such anecdotal evidence can be multiplied across the country, but what it means is that ministers are frequently being faced with the question of how far they should go in accommodating those who come to churches for special occasions and want to construct the liturgy using their own content. These are pastoral judgements where the minister is faced with deciding whether responding to the requests of families is more important than sticking to some rules or conventions that mean nothing to the people involved. People or rules?

Not exactly a new dilemma, but one being played out in a new cultural context which creates new blurred encounters.

There is a further dimension to these though. Such encounters can, and arguably should become the occasion for deeper reflection and analysis. What is happening here and how is one to make the appropriate pastoral judgement? This is where we are taken beyond the immediate pastoral response and into the realms of theological reflection.

Blurred encounters in the world

Similar dilemmas arise when Christians take on roles in a voluntary capacity, let alone in their actual places of work. It is becoming more difficult to express one's faith openly especially in a culture that sees people of faith as somehow eccentric or even dangerous. Hence the challenge is to know how explicit to be about a Christian commitment in working alongside others who do not share it. In recent years there have been well-publicized examples in the press of believers who have been put under pressure because they have displayed or worn some artefact related to their Christian faith, even though they may not have been engaging in open discussion of their beliefs.

Even within apparently more explicitly Christian organizations, such as Church schools, it can be difficult for Foundation governors appointed by either parish or diocese to maintain their values in the face of a largely secular culture where decisions are made according to financial criteria, or along the lines determined by the Education Authorities. In the case of the appointment of new teachers, for instance, should one favour a candidate because of their religious persuasion, or rather because they are the best candidate for the post even though their faith commitment is either vague or non-existent? If Church Aided schools could draw only upon a pool of teachers, or indeed Foundation governors who held explicit and clear Christian commitments, then there would be a real shortage of candidates. What happens in practice is that teachers and governors are appointed whose relationship to the Church is often tenuous to say the least, and then those of a stronger faith position quickly discover that the real drivers of decision are more secular and commercial values. The boundaries here are blurred by this range of beliefs, but hopefully all will still share the goal of doing what is best for the children and for that particular school community.

A biblical example

The parable of the Good Samaritan (Luke 10.29–37) contains elements that resonate with the idea of blurred encounters. The traveller from Jerusalem to Jericho takes a risk by making the journey in the first place, but is then set upon by thieves and left for dead at the roadside. The first person to pass is a priest, but he ignores the stricken traveller and continues on his way. The second is a Levite, and he does likewise. It is only the Samaritan who comes across and tends the wounds of the victim, sets him on his own beast, takes him to the nearest inn and then pays for him to be looked after. A number of boundaries are crossed. First, the boundary of personal risk which means that the Samaritan could be walking into a trap, but he nevertheless responds and offers help. Then the boundary of culture and convention which would expect the Samaritan to keep his distance and continue on his journey. Finally, the boundary between responding from love and compassion and the pragmatic response of looking out for one's own safety first. In the language used later in the book, the Samaritan is prepared to enter the liminal or uncertain space where the normal rules no longer apply and anything could happen. But it is only when a person is brave enough to do this that it becomes clear who one's neighbour is.

Different types of blurring

Physical boundaries

Boundaries of all sorts are blurred in ways not experienced in previous cultures. Perhaps the prime examples are in the threats to security posed by such phenomena as nuclear accidents, climate change, terrorist activity organized on a global scale and also food security. The rapid growth and ease of global travel and the scope of the internet have made national geographical boundaries more readily fluid and porous. Just in case this appears to have nothing to do with faith-based activity, consider the way in which many ministers now use email in order to help couples organize wedding services and to communicate about other church activities. Consider also the fact that many people now live their lives in different places and not just where they happen to have a point of residence, so their regular presence and therefore commitment to a particular geographical locality is often under question. The whole concept of the parish, village, circuit or county now means something different but the churches continue to base their structures and organization on the old patterns of residence and presence. As I have argued elsewhere (Reader, 2008), many of these categories of church and community life are now best seen as 'zombie categories', still functioning but only just, and largely out of touch with current lifestyles.

Ideological boundaries

Another related blurring is evident in the range of cultures and sub-cultures now to be found in specific localities. The presence of those of other faiths and of none alongside pockets of more traditional faith activity is common across countries such as the UK. As institutional religion continues to decline, the pressure to combine with those of other denominations increases and in certain places closer cooperation despite apparent doctrinal differences appears to be the logical way forward. Both beliefs and practices become blurred as this movement progresses. Yet this is to underestimate existing and more long-standing cultural differences both within and between communities. As many ministers will bear witness, particular congregations often have their own sub-culture of which they may not even be aware. It is only when a new minister arrives that he or she realizes that there are peculiarities associated with a specific group or place and that a challenge is to understand these and to learn how to work with them – or possibly against them!

Then of course there is the crossing of boundaries for those of faith who work in secular institutions and organizations and who face the challenge of working out how to exercise their faith within that context. As the wider culture becomes not simply more ignorant of but also openly hostile towards faith positions, the difficulties of negotiating this boundary become more acute. One can no longer take it for granted that one will gain a fair hearing or a sympathetic reception if one brings Christianity into the discussion.

Psychological boundaries

As the above may suggest, much depends on whether or not people learn how to handle themselves and their feelings within such encounters. Self-awareness and levels of reflexivity go alongside this willingness to be open to change and to see the world with different eyes. A blurring of boundaries requires a confidence and being comfortable with oneself that is not easily gained. Yet as more people learn to play different roles both at work and in their own time and also encounter others who differ in significant respects, then the greater flexibility of character may come more easily. A solid and static sense of identity can be a source of strength, but in a globalized culture the capacity to be more adaptable and open is more likely to enable effective relationships. To what extent though does this mean compromise for those of faith? An understanding of growth and faith development seems critical for the blurring of boundaries required at the psychological level.

Boundaries with other disciplines

One of the greatest challenges to those of faith is whether they are willing and able to access the resources of other disciplines as they enter such blurred encounters. Some theological reflection is all too eager to 'close the loop' as quickly as possible by bringing its own traditional resources into the equation, so one ends up back where one started having learnt nothing or not having made a creative contribution to the task in hand. Theology either has to have all the answers or to have the final word. If this is not to be the case however, there have to be some guidelines or rules of engagement between theology and other disciplines. Suffice it to say that theology is not the only discipline facing this challenge. How to relate the different sciences to politics, both to economics, let alone all to particular forms of ethical thought, is a major contemporary issue that few as yet have been willing to address (Latour, 2004). Latour works in an area that he calls Science Studies, looking among other things at the complex ways in which scientific research operates in practice and the means by which decisions are made about high-level problems such as nuclear power. He argues that the processes of decision making are inherently complicated and involve a number of factors: people, culture, things, beliefs and values as well as the supposedly 'rational' and objective facts that we often claim are at the heart of such decisions.

Latour's proposes that the idea of truth as itself the process of circulating references seems to be a creative and helpful way of describing the means by which decisions come about, and this seems to be consistent with the blurred encounters approach. One can see this from much more down-to-earth settings such as parents now having to exercise choice about where their children should go to school. How does one make such a decision? There are OfSTED reports to be consulted; school visits to be made; other parents to be listened to; questions of travel and finance to be considered; the issue of how many after-school activities are made available, let alone what seems best for this particular child and which school will be attended next. How much of this actually relates to 'objective facts of the case' and how much is more to do with feelings, the influence of others or of one's own schooling experience? At some point a decision has to be reached, but perhaps it is responsible to keep all the references circulating for as long as possible until that moment arrives?

An issue for theology is who decides what is the truth or 'the facts of the case' and on what grounds the references are to be stopped from circulating. The motto of blurred encounters should be 'keep the references circulating', and the aim to keep feeding new ideas and activities into the mix, including the insights from other disciplines that can inform our practice. In this way the liminal spaces required for personal faith development can be brought into play and opportunities for new and creative pastoral responses be encouraged.

Strategic choices

If there is to be genuine encounter – and by this we mean the possibility that either or both parties will be changed in the process – then it is essential that one must be prepared to let go of or abandon certain firmly held views or positions. This may be viewed as compromise, or it might be part of a process of negotiation whereby a new truth emerges from the process itself. Can there be real learning, growth or development for individuals and communities, or indeed within relationships, unless the possibility of such change remains open? If all such encounters can only be conducted on the terms of one of the parties, or provided that the other comes round to my way of thinking and accepts that 'I am in the right', then this is simply what has been called an 'ethics of appropriation', or an imperialistic approach to the encounter (Reader, 2005). Much faith-based apparent crossing of boundaries is of this nature and does not count as a genuine encounter. In the genuine blurred encounter you have to be prepared to take the risk of letting go or revising previously held positions.

Concluding commentary

This chapter has emphasized the importance of a trigger to generate the energy and commitment needed for a process of theological reflection to begin. In this case, the trigger came not from a shared context but from an idea drawn from the writings of one of the authors, John Reader. This blurred encounters idea proved sufficient to bring together the people we wanted in order to have the conversation which we felt was missing from the life of the Church. Sometimes attempts at theological reflection are abortive because the energy and commitment is not built in the group. Time spent exploring the basis for the conversation and trying out the trigger on intended participants is time well spent. We were blessed by energetic and open-minded participants who were willing to reflect together.

3

Describing the Encounters

Introductory commentary

As Chapter 1 explained, it is customary for theological reflection to start with descriptions of concrete experience. We had asked participants to reflect on the idea of blurred encounters and submit an incident from their own experience which they felt illustrated the idea. Circulating these descriptions before the event helped participants feel they were on the same page. It enabled them to start to empathize with each other's work and find points of connection despite coming from different parts of the country and having different occupations or ministries.

Description can sometimes become the Cinderella of theological reflection. That which is put to one side once the more glamorous work of exploration and reflection starts. However, unlike the natural or social sciences, the things that we seek to describe in Christian practice have often not been described before. Attention to whose voices inform the description, what elements are put in the foreground and which in the background can help tease out from the practitioner the richness of their practice before any wider exploration commences.

What we discovered during the event is that those who are committed to their own context and practice are keen to absorb what they can of the context and practice of others. The significance of a telling detail is understood. The limitations of their observations are respected and probed. The example of the Emmaus Road story used in Chapter 1, reminds us that we can do nothing but describe the situation as we understand it, at this time and in this company. Sympathetic questions will draw us out and prepare us for the next step in the process.

The structure of the chapter

This chapter offers examples of the 'blurred encounters' introduced in Chapter 2. The encounters are grouped into three clusters focusing in turn on professional–client relationships, experiences in organizations and experiences in communities. These distinctions are made to help readers locate the types of encounter that might be most relevant to their experience. Chapters 4 and 6 use the same clusters to explore the encounters and then finally learn from them for future practice.

Experiences in professional–client relationships

The first three encounters presented come from the world of professional–client relationships. They show how those relationships can become blurred and the complex web of relationships within which they are set.

ENCOUNTER 1: The General Practitioner and the drug addict

David is a GP who worked for several years in a community prescribing clinic for drugs addiction, mostly dealing with heroin addicts. Darren is one of the patients with whom David worked at the clinic. Darren has a heroin and crack cocaine habit dating back about ten years. For the past five years

David has been treating Darren for his addiction, and Darren had been doing well. He was employed, worked hard at his job and was married with two young daughters. In addition to his addiction, Darren also suffers with bipolar disorder and takes additional medication to stabilize his mood.

Three months ago things began to go wrong for Darren when he came across an old friend who was a drug dealer. This encounter led to a brush with the police concerning a stolen car, which precipitated a spiral back into the regular use of heroin and cocaine. Fed by heroin and cocaine, Darren's behaviour became erratic. Eventually his wife gave him an ultimatum: stop taking drugs or move out. Unable to muster the resolve to keep away from heroin, Darren did move out, and the family split up. Darren ended up living in a rented room; he believes that he has no hope for reconciliation and deeply misses his wife and daughters. As a consequence of this circumstance, his mood is low. In an attempt to seek consolation and to find some 'escape' from his tragedy, Darren returned to using drugs and now uses them even more than before.

After working with Darren for five years and seeing how he had been able to establish some stability in his life, David feels that he is now watching a man throw away his marriage and family. To David, Darren's return to drug taking seems like a form of adultery: Darren has been seduced by drugs away from his wife. Although Darren wants to be reconciled with his family, the hold of his other 'love', heroin, is too captivating. Darren is unable to see any hope in the situation and in his experience heroin now offers the one form of 'consolation' that he is able to access in his desolation.

In this encounter, as a professional David has had to witness the breakdown of his patient's life from relative stability and social integration into painful chaos and social isolation. From a professional point of view, he feels unable to offer any interventions that might alter the situation or reverse the painful trajectory of disintegration. David has supported Darren for five years and has felt some satisfaction in seeing him establish a relatively stable way of life. Seeing this stability crumble raises mixed feelings of sadness, confusion, anger and frustration and poses several fundamental questions: What is my role in such a situation? Who should I be for this person in pain? What have I to offer this person in my professional capacity as a doctor and how does that relate to who I am as a person and as a person of faith? What does this situation require of me both as a professional and as a person of faith? How should I respond to the challenges that this encounter throws up for me? What professional, personal and theological resources can I draw on in order to act with integrity in this situation?

At the time, David felt a deep frustration with Darren and with the events that had taken place. After all the hard work it has come to this! It seemed to David that the options he had were: he could try to motivate Darren; he could continue to support him; he could challenge him in an appropriate way. However, as the encounter continued David could see little sign of change or of hope. He recognized that, 'Fundamentally, I cannot change his heart.'

The encounter challenged David to reflect on 'What really is my role in this encounter? Am I a doctor, a parent, a friend, a judge?' The encounter challenged clear-cut professional boundaries engaging David personally as well as professionally and as a person of faith: the encounter became blurred. What emerged was the realization for David that from his professional point of view, it was no longer easy to see how he had any more control or power than Darren in this situation. The encounter had brought him to a different place altogether, one where the resources he might need to draw upon were of a different order to the technical resources of medicine. David knew that he could not impose a solution; that would never work and any attempt to do so would not only be unethical but would damage the therapeutic relationship that he had built up with Darren. He had to accept that all he could do now was to create as far as possible a positive context within which to encourage change – and wait and hope.

ENCOUNTER 2: The minister and the cancer patient

Tom is an Anglican priest and a trained counsellor. Mark was a nineteen year old young man who was having chemotherapy treatment for bone cancer. Mark's parents were concerned that Mark had appropriate support at this extremely difficult time and they asked Tom if he would visit their son. Tom agreed to visit. When he called to see Mark he was at one of the low points of the cycle of chemotherapy. Mark was clearly feeling despair and anger, feelings expressed in this initial encounter with Tom. Mark had never experienced such awful depths in his life and Tom could understand that he should feel as he did.

Sometime later, when the cycle of treatment had finished and the cancer was in remission, Mark was feeling much better. He contacted Tom in order to apologize to him for how short tempered he must have seemed during his visit. Tom assured him that he understood how difficult things were for him at the time and that he had no difficulty with him at all. A year and a half later, Mark contacted Tom again. He told Tom that the disease had progressed and that he was likely to die of his condition in the next few months. He asked Tom if he could meet to talk with him and they arranged to do so.

At this second meeting, Mark explained that he was not a Christian and in fact, that he did not believe in God. However, he would like his funeral service to be held in church and he would like Tom to take it. It was clear from this request that Mark trusted the relationship that had been established between himself and Tom based as it was on acceptance, understanding and respect. Tom felt very honoured to be asked to take the service and he told Mark how he felt. Mark was concerned that the service should have integrity; he wanted nothing to be said on his behalf which suggested that he had a Christian belief. However, he recognized that there would be people present who did have a Christian faith and he was very happy for things to be said that would speak to them. Having discussed the service, Tom and Mark walked across to the church. Tom found it terribly poignant to walk into the church with Mark in the expectation that the next occasion on which he would enter, would be at his funeral.

When Mark eventually died, bearing in mind the conversations they had shared and wanting to honour Mark's wishes, Tom discussed every detail of the service very carefully with his family. They too wanted fully to honour his wishes. The focal point of the discussions became the words of commendation. These are the words used by the priest to commend the deceased person to God's eternal care in Christ. Everyone knew that Mark would not have wished such an entreaty to be made on his behalf; it was clearly inappropriate. Instead of these words, Tom agreed with the family that at this crucial point of the service he would say: 'And now we wish Mark well on his journey.' He was glad to find a form of expression that respected the integrity of Mark's wishes and beliefs. At the same time, the words were able to draw all those present into a well-wishing for him in a statement that expressed some (undefined) hope for his continuing journey and not his end. While not overtly Christian, Tom felt that he too could use these words with integrity. The service 'worked' well and the family and those who attended expressed satisfaction with what had taken place. Thinking about the experience, Tom reflected that it is possible that the carefully thought through form of the service enabled him to meet with those who attended across many spiritual boundaries even more than if it had been a straightforwardly Christian service. People recognized and appreciated the respect for Mark's belief that had been shown in the careful planning and taking of the service.

In this encounter, Tom was faced with challenges on several levels. The experience as a whole challenged and moved him deeply and this is reflected in the fact that it stayed with him for many years. As a trained counsellor, his initial encounter with Mark drew attention to the boundaries between listening, counselling and pastoral care. However, Tom was also aware that the encounter was significant on a far deeper spiritual level than this.

As a person trained and experienced in counselling and pastoral care, Tom was able to understand and to empathize with the pain that this young man was experiencing when they first met. In making himself available to Mark and in accepting him as he was, a relationship of trust was established. When Mark subsequently approached Tom with the request that he take his funeral but without imputing to him any Christian belief, Tom had to decide how to respond to this request. It raised the question for Tom of how to respect with integrity the spirituality of everyone concerned: Mark, his family and friends and his own Christian faith. In working this out in genuine dialogue with the family, Tom moved beyond any need to hold rigid boundaries that might have insisted on a totally orthodox Christian funeral service. He understood that such a course might have alienated those present and would certainly have violated the relationship that had been established with Mark. Instead he risked being in a place of genuine openness and encounter that met the needs of those involved and potentially spoke to them of the inclusive and unconditional love of God.

ENCOUNTER 3: The head teacher and the informal foster carer

Pat is the Head Teacher at a Church of England primary school. A few months ago, one of the families with children at the school lost their home and had to go into accommodation that Social Services found for them. There had been difficulties within the family for some time. Sally, the mother, lived with her two older children from her first marriage. The eldest daughter began secondary school in September 2009, and the eldest son attends Pat's school. During the last 18 months, two more children had been born, and Sally made plans to remarry. Although the family was struggling financially, Sally went ahead with plans for the wedding and the marriage took place. It is probably the case that the expense of the wedding was met from the home finances with the loss of the house as a consequence. The family move would mean that the two older children would have to change schools.

Sally's neighbour Jean recognized the importance of continuity in education and was concerned for the welfare of the two eldest siblings. Although Jean has a partner and two children of her own, she offered to take Sally's two eldest children into her own home so that they could continue their education at their current schools.

Sally agreed to the proposal, and an arrangement began on an informal basis. Jean took out a bank loan in order to help cover the costs of caring for two additional children. Social Services are now seeking to 'regularize' this arrangement by putting the children on the 'looked after' register. In effect, Jean has taken on the role of informal foster parent. She has limited education herself but Pat has found it humbling to meet with her and to see how she has been willing to provide for someone else's children as part of her own family. In her down-to-earth manner, Jean provides what these children very much needed: a stable environment with firm boundaries to help them feel secure. Sally does visit her children but not on a regular basis. Jean ensures that Sally turns up to parents evenings at the school, but it is Jean who assesses homework, listens to the children read and provides the guidelines that give some security and order to their disrupted lives.

As head teacher with a concern for the pastoral care and wellbeing of all the children in her school, Pat is in regular contact with Jean. She has been very much impressed by the way in which Jean has given so generously of herself in caring for Sally's children. No one can forecast how long the arrangement will continue, but the situation causes Pat to reflect that she knows of very few people who would be as generous and selfless as to open their home to children who have been perceived as 'difficult'.

Jean's response to the situation that her neighbour's children find themselves in engages Pat simultaneously as a person of faith and as a professional teacher. It challenges Pat to make her own response. As a Christian person, Pat sees Jean's response to the situation as an example of Christian love in action. She sees how beneficial it has been to the children to be provided with a stable home environment, and she supports Jean in her generous and genuine offer of hospitality. However, as a professional, Pat is also aware of the risk involved in such an act of generous giving. She knows that this kind of loving involvement characteristically involves risk. The situation leads her to ask the question: 'Where will it end?' To this, of course, there is no answer. One could say that, in a very real sense, Pat's decision to support Jean in her course of action is an act of faith. It is in the indeterminacy of the situation, involving the vulnerable lives of young children, that the blurred encounter finds its primary locus. Having come to trust, and perhaps even to love Jean, Pat knows that if the informal fostering arrangement fails for some reason, the children will be very vulnerable and possibly lost without Jean.

Experiences in organizations

This section explores the accounts of lay Christians and ministers working in organizations and identifies some of the blurred encounters that emerged during the small group discussions. It will become clear that these refer to a range of different contexts and experiences, but that common themes begin to surface even at this early stage in the process.

ENCOUNTER 1: How email can dominate our lives

In the first of two accounts we learn of the experiences of a consultant operating in the business environment, and who has particular expertise in the field of organizational behaviour. His starting point is that well-led and well-structured organizations with well-designed systems can be good places for human beings to express their potential and to gain self-esteem. The specific issue that he then raises however, is that of the role of email within the work context.

Having attended a course for middle managers from a large scientific organization, the participants were asked to communicate about the homework they were to do before the next session. The consultant suggested that they do so by email using the joining instructions email, which contained all the addresses. The response to this was illuminating and revealed the way in which email has now become all-pervasive and intrusive to the point where it becomes a barrier to effective communication. Two people simply laughed at the consultant's suggestion and said that there was no way they would still have an email sent a week earlier. Given that they receive something like 500 emails a day, their inboxes have to be junked frequently in order to prevent them overloading. This impression was reinforced by the fact that most participants at the conference checked their blackberries at every available moment in order to deal with their emails.

The consequence of this is that middle managers such as these are afforded no time or space to recover from work demands, or even to interact effectively with fellow participants at a conference. Their minds and attention are always elsewhere, responding to the next tranche of messages requiring their concentration. While this was described as a real burden and a source of stress, it was also worn as a 'badge of pride' by many. The more emails one receives the more important one must be within the organization! So there appears to be a perverse psychology at work here. On the one hand, the incessant demands issuing from the technology inhibits face-to-face communication, but it is also seen as some sort of substitute for it as individuals vie for the prize of most connected employee.

What does this tell us about individuals working in organizations and also about human community, given the growing role of information technology? There is no doubt that email is a useful technology, allowing quick, cheap and accessible communication across time zones. But the requirement for universal access, meaning that one is on demand 24 hours a day, interrupts other relationships and attention spans. There is a danger of unengaged interaction, so an email is sent without any knowledge of the receiver's status or state of being and with the assumption that the other shares the sense of urgency of the sender and will respond as quickly as possible. There is often frustration when the other fails to respond within a certain limited time span. There is little of the accountability, negotiation or reciprocity that comes from a face-to-face or even a telephone encounter.

The pressures created heighten when the message comes from a superior, authority figure, or customer and mistakes in communication become dangerous or misleading. Without being able to read the body language in a direct encounter it is easy to misinterpret the tone of what is being communicated. Hence the general consequence of using a technology that is now essential and taken for granted in many organizations, is that the human dimensions of encounter are not taken into account. At its worst then, email in human organizations produces stress, dehumanization and broken community.

Although this may appear to be a very technical and narrow experience within the organizational world, it is now so common as to require deeper reflection and analysis. As becomes clear from this encounter, it raises questions about human relationships and interaction, and indeed about the nature of community in the work environment. 'There is no escape' from email and constant communication, but what is the quality of this contact and what is the consequence for both sender and receiver? What is on the surface a 'good thing' rapidly turns into something more blurred and ambiguous.

ENCOUNTER 2: The contrast between church and business

The second encounter again emerges from somebody highly experienced in an organizational context, but also with a formal role in his local church as a churchwarden. This leads to some interesting and challenging reflections on the contrast between the two. The actual details of the work context need to remain confidential, but suffice it to say that they are from an academic and scientific research establishment where our contributor is both a scientist and a team manager. The church context is a medium-sized Anglican church. The question that begins to emerge is that of whether the person concerned operates in the same way in both contexts, or whether there are tensions and differences between the two roles.

The initial reflection is that there should not, in principle, be any difference in terms of management style and approach. At least, just because one setting is secular and the other religious, there does not need to be clear differentiation. The same values and attitudes should apply in both. It is the expectations, however, that appear to create differences. One of course is a paid environment, while the other is voluntary. This is a significant difference that demands deeper exploration. The focus of this reflection though is on differences in values and in consequent management styles.

In the secular setting there is an expectation of a certain 'robustness', and the feeling that 'this isn't a democracy', and also that it is good to be seen to be very busy the whole time. When changes are made in the organization, the focus is upon the final objectives and less on the impact upon the people involved. So the journey that people are making themselves is not given much thought or attention as the main consideration is implementing the changes as swiftly and efficiently as possible.

In the church setting, by contrast, this idea of managerial robustness is not seen as being so appropriate. The emphasis is rather upon community unity or taking people with you when changes are being considered. This often makes change harder to achieve of course, as a lack of consensus is seen as a reason for not moving forward. Once again, this is obviously a difference between paid and voluntary activity, and means that the management style in the latter has to be less coercive and more persuasive. Another difference is that contemplative pursuits can be preferred over those requiring action or activity.

A further question that arises from this is over the nature of change and how this happens – or doesn't happen – in different contexts. In the organizational world, change management is well established as an approach and discipline, and the assumption is that change is a constant in business life. Change in a church setting is of a very different order, is much harder to achieve and takes much longer. There are theological reasons for this, potentially at least, in that the recall to tradition and authority are much more prevalent in a religious context. The presumption is more likely to be of continuity and respect for the past, whereas in most other organizations it is probably of change and development. Yet perhaps there are values and insights from both sides of the divide that could be of benefit to the other. This is the tentative conclusion of this participant as he reflects upon his blurred encounter between local church and the research establishment.

Experiences in communities

This final set of blurred encounters come from the world of community engagement where Christian practitioners are seeking to change structures alongside engaging with individual needs.

ENCOUNTER 1: Encounter between a faith-based charity and the NHS

Luke works for a small but well-established faith-based charity in a London borough. The charity provides a range of services but is always keen to learn from clients about the underlying social problems in the area and how they might be tackled. It provides two separate services, a free bereavement counselling service and a cold weather shelter for rough sleepers. It decided to take part in a community research project looking at the connections between bereavement and homelessness. The borough contains extremes of wealth and poverty, is highly diverse and has a considerable turnover in its population.

The Bereavement Service referred Julie as one of their clients willing to take part in the research. Luke agreed to meet Julie and introduce her to Kirsty the researcher. He learned that she had just become homeless so when they met at 9 am he completed the shelter guest registration form to gain information about her housing situation. He then left Julie with Kirsty for the research interview, while he went to make some phone calls about her housing needs.

About 15 minutes into the interview, Kirsty asked Luke to contact Julie's GP and make an immediate appointment as she had become extremely distraught and was expressing suicidal thoughts. Julie's GP offered an appointment for 11.45am. Kirsty and Luke accompanied Julie to the GP who decided to refer her to the North Borough Mental Health Crisis Team. The GP was unable to get a response from the Crisis Team and so it was agreed with Julie that she would return with Luke and Kirsty to the charity's office and wait there. The GP felt strongly that, for her own safety, Julie should not return to her son's flat.

With no contact from the Crisis Team, Luke made further telephone calls including to the GP. The Crisis Team claimed that because her current residence was in a neighbouring borough, they would have to refer her to their Crisis Team. Luke insisted that her son's address was in their area. After checking they reluctantly agreed it was in their borough but fell under the South Borough Crisis Team. The GP would need to make a referral call to them. By now it was 2 pm, and Julie was becoming increasingly distraught.

Eventually the North Borough Crisis Team agreed to take the referral but said that it was now too late in the day for the team to come out to assess Julie. They suggested that Luke take Julie to the hospital A&E for assessment. Thankfully

Julie agreed to this and Kirsty and Luke accompanied her. A member of the hospital psychiatric team conducted an assessment. The room in which the assessment took place was awful – pretty much like a police holding cell. No thought seemed to be given to the effect of the surroundings on Julie.

After the lengthy hospital assessment interview, the psychiatrist said that they would admit Julie to a local crisis bed for the night and that the Crisis Team would meet with her the next day. Luke and Kirsty checked that Julie was comfortable with this proposal. She had been keeping family and friends updated on her mobile phone. She was happy to have somewhere safe to stay for the night. Luke made sure she knew how to make contact with the charity again should she need to. Luke and Kirsty left the hospital – it was nearly 6 pm.

An unintended consequence of the charity's desire to understand the community in which it was working was that Luke and Kirsty spent a whole day gaining a detailed understanding of what it was like to be both homeless and have mental health difficulties in their community. The theme of the day was poor communication between the different parts of the NHS. Luke and Kirsty reflected on how important good communication was both to the bereavement counselling service and the cold weather shelter the charity ran. People whose lives were disrupted by bereavement needed more than the ten-minute consultation a GP was able to offer. People who were sleeping rough needed more than a bed for the night; they needed hospitality, a place where they were treated like a guest rather than a series of problems to be solved. They speculated about what would have happened to Julie if they had not been available at the time of her crisis. They had in effect been the 'crisis team' setting aside the other work they had planned that day and extending their working day until Julie's situation had been engaged with by those in a position to deal with her most urgent need – her mental health needs.

Luke identified this as a blurred encounter because it raised questions about how his voluntary organization should respond when faced with a client who had needs they could not meet. It also raised confusing questions about the relationship between his organization and the health service. The charity wanted to have positive relationships with the local health service but was disturbed by what it had learned about its ability to respond to someone undergoing a mental health crisis. Did it have a responsibility to challenge the system? Had they done the right thing in setting aside their work for the day? Should they just have taken Julie to A&E when they left the GP's surgery in the morning?

This case illustrates some of the difficulties faced by voluntary sector workers trying to understand the context in which their clients live, in order to provide more effective services. Deciding to spend time trying to conduct research, they end up spending time responding to an individual in crisis, something which the NHS systems designed for that purpose seem unable to do in a timely and compassionate manner.

ENCOUNTER 2: Encounter between a vicar and the media in a community regeneration project

Pauline is vicar of a parish on a large deprived outer estate in one of the Home Counties. The estate is used as a pool of social housing to relocate problematic households. It has poor public transport connections with the nearest town and so residents are dependent upon services on the estate. It is an almost entirely white population with a lot of long-term worklessness and many residents having multiple problems. Having an address on the estate is sufficient to stigmatize residents in the eyes of employers and service-providers. Pauline works with most local agencies including police, social services, district and county councils, schools and GPs. This encounter tracks the connection between an attempt to regenerate the estate and the impact on the life of one resident.

Pauline invited a television company onto the estate to make a series of 'The Choir', a BBC2 series in which an outside conductor forms a Community Choir and coaches them to a public performance – the process being filmed as a documentary. Pauline's aim in inviting the TV company in was to give the local community something to feel proud of and to remove the negative perceptions of the estate. No amount of physical regeneration had changed the image of the estate and its residents as 'a waste of space'.

The choir was, and still is, made up of many members of the community, including those with chaotic lives. One choir member, Steve, had misused both drugs and alcohol and had mental health issues. On joining the choir he became determined to stay clean of both alcohol and drugs and achieved this for many months. However, he developed a zeal for telling his story and recounting his problems as an alcoholic. He was one of the programme's 'characters' and was, therefore, filmed at length on a number of occasions. The director and producer were sensitive and would confer with Pauline about how Steve was coping with the filming.

During one filming session he poured out his heart about his life – particularly the history of alcoholism in his family, which had directly led to the death of his mother and brother. Steve rang Pauline and said that he felt the cameraman had just left without helping him to recover from recalling such painful memories. The director rang Pauline and asked for her views about using the footage. She pointed out that Steve and his children would have to live with the consequences if his story went out on national television. The footage was never used.

A few weeks later, Pauline was called out of a choir rehearsal and told that Steve had phoned the producer and said he was about to commit suicide. The young cameraman stopped filming and took Pauline and the producer round to Steve's house. They called the police and an ambulance and gained access to the house and helped Steve recover.

The film crew were part of the life of the estate for many months. During that time they witnessed many serious pastoral situations but they retained their emphasis on sensitivity to the lives of the residents. Although the TV series is finished, Steve is still a member of the choir and still clean of drugs and alcohol.

Pauline told this story as a blurred encounter because it showed her taking a professional risk by involving the media with a deprived community containing vulnerable people. The power of the media in legitimating a group of people and telling a story which would otherwise remain untold is huge in contemporary culture. This legitimation acted both on the community from which the choir was drawn but also on those individuals and organizations that have both the power to stigmatize it and to provide much-needed resources for its regeneration. However, the power of the media carries risks. These include, that power will be used in a way that damages those whose stories are told. That ethical boundaries will be transgressed particularly when dealing with people who may not always be in a position to have regard for their own best interests. In the work of community regeneration, resources are most usually put into physical and economic regeneration, ignoring the social or spiritual regeneration that are needed if the community is to gain a positive identity. The use of the media gave a story of success to the community – a chance to step back and see itself through a lens that while trying to dramatize was not trying to stigmatize. How can such a risk be evaluated? If the consequences for Steve had not been positive, would that have been attributed to the involvement of the media? Why was it that other forms of treatment and support had failed to have a similarly regenerating effect on Steve? Why was it that other forms of regeneration had not had a similarly galvanizing effect on the perceptions of the estate?

ENCOUNTER 3: Encounter between a regeneration worker and a housing association board

Philip is a lawyer with 20 years' experience of the legal issues that have arisen in regeneration initiatives across the country. He is also active in a charity which trains people to work in regeneration initiatives and deal confidently with the multiple stakeholders they involve.

Philip was asked by a large Housing Association to help them complete a review of their governance structures. The Association had a majority of directors who were residents in its properties. The desire was to secure a significant set of changes with the support of all key stakeholders. These included the management and staff of the Association, residents, 13 constituent groups reflecting the demographic composition of the residents, 11 neighbourhood groups representing the communities in which the housing stock was located and the existing board, which included local politicians and business representatives as well as the majority of residents.

The review process revealed a number of issues. Some long-term directors needed to come to terms with the fact that their terms of office had expired and they needed to retire from the board; the desire of community leaders to secure the future wellbeing of the Association alongside their scepticism that suitable new directors could be found; different levels of ability, trust and mutual understanding between existing board members; the fact that key decision makers came from different faith communities and had different ambitions for the Association.

These internal issues had to be grappled with while facing the reality of a changing external environment with growing regulatory requirements, with pressures on local authorities regarding the fair allocation of housing, and with the growing legal complexities facing housing associations. As facilitator, Philip felt the pressure of working with a Housing Association that had the reputation of being pioneering with a desire that the outcome should be groundbreaking.

His role was to be the all-listening person taking in the hopes, fears and frustrations of all the stakeholders. Throughout the 18 months of working with them, he identified the following challenges:

- Creating the right environment for dialogue by facilitating discussions.
- Dealing with the history of the organization as perceived by the different stakeholders.
- Discerning which issues to leave, which to pursue urgently and which to let flow.
- How to be accountable and transparent when much of the information gained was through relationships of trust.
- Constantly assessing both the risk and the potential gain.

The ultimate outcome was an agreed set of changes that have taken the organization into a new era.

Reflecting on this prolonged encounter, Philip saw it as a blurred encounter because it was a test not only of his technical expertise and skill in facilitating a process but also of his spiritual integrity gaining and not abusing trust; being like a steward in taking risks rather than burying difficult issues being both as wise as serpents and as innocent as doves. It wasn't possible to retain a professional identity alone. He had to show that he was aware of the stakes for the organization in working out its values – his identity as a person of faith played its part in this. In listening to the voices of multiple stakeholders he had to retain his own identity as an outsider able to offer honest feedback to the organization about both its internal workings and its external context. He also felt in all of this a need to understand the communities the Housing Association served and the vital role played by good quality, well-managed social housing in regenerating disadvantaged communities. Governance is more than a technical issue; it is the means by which the purposes and values of an organization are sustained. If this Housing Association was to continue as a leader in its field, it needed effective ways of sustaining the support of its stakeholders while having the freedom to innovate.

Concluding commentary

We noticed when we came to write up the book that the group focusing on professional–client relationships and the group focusing on communities discussed specific instances whereas the group focusing on organizations came up with examples that could have occurred in many contexts. We don't wish to read any particular significance into this, other than to note that the dynamics in any small group will take it on its own journey. Where theological reflection processes allow a larger group to break down into smaller groups it is worth considering how much direction the small groups need and whether a range of approaches will enhance or inhibit the wider task.

4

Exploring the Encounters

Introductory commentary

Having described their experiences to each other, participants were invited to look for common themes which they
felt emerged from their experiences. Again, this is different
from the use of the pastoral cycle to explore a single situation where the exploration phase might involve turning to a
different discipline or gathering more information about the
particular context. Here the aim was to bring people into conversation to discern if there is anything of significance which
their experiences have in common. These were exploratory
discussions that ranged far and wide but in the end each group
was asked to summarize their discussion in three themes. As
in the previous chapter, the themes have been clustered using
the categories of professional–client relationships, organizations and communities. We suggest you continue to read the
cluster that interests you most.

Emerging themes in professional–client relationships

THEME 1: Exploring the relationship between role and self

The three encounters in the previous chapter concerned a
medical, a religious and an educational professional. All three

practitioners had high levels of training and a great deal of experience in their field. They were equipped with practical and theoretical knowledge and with ethical and legal frameworks within which to work. As professionals, they are aware of the appropriate boundaries to set and also that in most circumstances, they are the ones with the power to set the agenda and with the resources that they need to draw upon in order to deal with a given situation. All of these professional resources are designed to minimize risk to both professional and client, to keep safe those who enter into a professional–client relationship by ensuring that the boundary between the professional and the personal is not transgressed. These safeguards are necessary and entirely appropriate. And yet, as experienced practitioners in the helping professions know, beyond all the technical expertise, one of the most powerful and effective sources of healing and transformation within professional relationships can be the willingness of the professional to engage in a genuine human encounter with the client and that in order to do that, the professional needs to be able to be themselves within their professional role. This was one of the main themes that emerged from reflection on the encounters.

The professional remains a person. In order to have integrity as a professional, a person needs to be aware of their own values and beliefs so that they can act in accordance with both their professional and their personal values and beliefs. In many situations, who you are is as important to the healing processes within a professional relationship as what one does: being present for the other can itself be a source of healing and transformation. In relation to this, a person's faith and spiritual beliefs are an important part of their self-identity. In the encounter between David and Darren for example, David had invested quite a lot of himself in supporting Darren over five years and he was aware of his own feelings of disappointment, sadness and frustration at having to witness the disintegration of so much that had been built. However, David also recognized that he no longer had any more resources to draw on from his professional 'toolkit'; what he had to offer Darren was his willingness to be present to him, to be in solidarity with him as another human being who cares about his wellbeing out of love. David characterized this as having a commitment to 'covenant' as distinct from 'contract' love. As a professional, David could have chosen to end his relationship with Darren when he returned to drug taking. As a person formed in the Christian faith, David understood his commitment to Darren as going beyond the honouring of a professional contract to having a continuing concern for him as a fellow human being created in the image of God.

Because David was open to this genuine human encounter, he was able to acknowledge and accept his own vulnerability beyond his professional identity, to take account of his own values and beliefs and to act in accordance with them in this professional context. In a very real sense, this human encounter threw David back on himself, forcing him to explore: the boundaries between the personal and the professional; his personal and professional identity; the relationship between his Christian faith and his professional life; the implications of his commitment to living in solidarity with God and humanity; his understanding of the Christian imperative to love one another as God loves us. David was left with the question: can professionalism allow passion to inform the therapeutic approach? That is 'passion' as the capacity to suffer and to 'suffer with' (compassion) and as the power of loving commitment that is willing to go beyond strict contractual obligations.

This same theme emerged in the encounter between head teacher Pat and foster parent Jean. As a person of faith, Pat identified Jean's generosity as Christian love in action, a sign of the breaking in of the kingdom, and it moved and humbled her to witness this. Pat supported Jean in her professional role, but the encounter spoke to her as a person and posed for her the same questions about the demands of love and the counter-cultural risk of loving in a social and professional climate that is risk averse.

For Tom, the religious professional, the encounter with Mark focused attention on the relationship between his professional identity as a minister and his Christian identity as a person. In order to be authentic in his professional role, Tom had to act with integrity both in relation to his own values and beliefs and to those of Mark. Out of his commitment to the demand of genuine love that the difference and integrity of the other is respected, Tom was able to negotiate the different demands of the self, the other and the professional role. In doing so, he risked compromise, misunderstanding and even failure but retained his own integrity within the encounter and within his professional role.

These encounters show that the professional role is complex and that it needs constant negotiation in the context of specific client relationships. They also show that who we are as persons with our particular world view, values and beliefs is part of who we are and how we work as professionals. Whether this is acknowledged or not, it is always part of the equation. The relationship between our self-identity as followers of Christ and our professional identity is central to the professional–client relationship. The above examples indicate the value of exploring this relationship in order to ensure that we act with integrity and remain faithful practitioners in whatever profession we work.

THEME 2: Discovering ways of knowing

Professional people, by definition are highly trained and educated, their identity formed in accordance with the body of theoretical and practical knowledge that constitutes the foundation of professional practice. A high value is placed upon the academic knowledge and cognitive learning that is the basis of professional competence. This is right and proper: we all want the professionals that we turn to for help or advice to be competent! However, because cognitive ways of knowing are valued so highly in western culture, it is easy to lose sight of the fact that there are different ways of knowing.

It is fascinating to note how this observation relates to the process of the group during its discussions about the encounters. Following extensive discussion about the emerging themes, the group at one point came to a consensus: foundational to all our thinking are the theological and doctrinal presuppositions that we hold about the nature of God and how God is involved in the life of the world. This is a reasonable thing to assert. It is natural for people who are theologically articulate to begin with their ideas about God and the world and then to reflect on their experience in the light of those ideas. However, as the discussion continued and the process unfolded further, a curious thing happened: as people continued to get more deeply in touch with the experience of being in the encounters, the focus of attention changed from ways of knowing *about God* to an exploration of ways of *knowing God* in their own experience. This led to a reformulation of what people considered to be foundational for their life and work: experience of and relationship with God. Knowing God took precedence over what they knew *about* God via the faith tradition. It seems that what the group was discovering for itself was the value that members placed on experiential knowing as distinct from cognitive knowing: the authority of experience took precedence over that of theology and doctrine.

This discovery of different orders of knowledge relates directly to the encounters that were being discussed. What people discovered was that genuine human encounters, if we allow them to question and challenge us, can be the source of a different order of knowledge. This knowledge of self and other is experiential and therefore seen as self-authenticating: I know this in my own experience. Access to this way of knowing requires us to be willing to be open to encounter the other. The basis for this encounter is genuine dialogue, which presupposes not only respect for difference, but openness to the possibility that the encounter may require us to change. This stance requires a good deal of self-knowledge and personal and spiritual maturity: preconceptions and images of the other need to be set aside in order to allow the reality of the other to be encountered. In the group discussions, although the connection was not explicitly made, it is not surprising that people's direct experience of God in their own lives was discussed at some length. Having the deeply affirming and healing experience of being known by God establishes our identity and provides the basis for our understanding of and way of being with and for others.

In the encounter between David and Darren, it is when David has come to the end of his strictly professional repertoire that he is forced to think about what it means to be with his client in the current circumstances and what he has to learn from this experience. Different things come into focus: the importance of presence and relationship; the demands of love and the preciousness of every human life; what faith means in this situation; how to bear witness in the face of suffering. In Pat's encounter with Jean, she is prepared to let go of her preconceptions about Jean as someone with limited education who might not be able to cope and in so doing encounters someone who teaches her about hospitality and the generosity of God at work in the world. In his encounter with Mark, Tom experiences trust and mutual respect across spiritual boundaries. By meeting the challenge that Mark poses, he is able to witness in his professional role to the unconditional love of God.

All these encounters bear witness to the fact that when people remained open to genuine encounter with others, with themselves and with God, they began to discover the spiritual, theological and therapeutic significance of different ways of knowing.

THEME 3: Living with uncertainty

On the whole, professionals are used to living with certainty. Their knowledge, expertise and experience means that, on one level, they expect to be able to draw on their considerable resources in order to work out an appropriate and helpful response that will make a difference in the client's situation. They are used to having power and control in the relationships they establish with clients and they are used to being fairly secure in their professional and role identity. However, because genuine human encounters are always unique and often unpredictable, they always carry an element of risk. We may expect a relationship to unfold in a certain way but we cannot guarantee that it will do so. Uncertainty and risk are built into human relating. This may be anxiety provoking in some situations but it is also a potential source of creativity, healing and growth. New things can emerge when people are willing to risk uncertainty and sooner or later, those engaged in the caring professions inevitably encounter situations which require of them the mature capacity to live with uncertainty.

This theme emerged strongly in all three encounters and in the group discussions. In his encounter with Darren, David found himself confronted with the apparent disintegration of the stable way of life that Darren had managed to establish with David's support. Any sense of certainty about the outcomes and efficacy of David's professional interventions is called into question by the actions that Darren takes. This development raises fundamental questions for David and forces him to live with uncertainty. In spite of all his professional knowledge, David is left with questions not answers: How might the situation unfold? What kind of response does this require of me? How does/could my faith inform my professional relationship? What have I to learn from this relationship? How does this encounter inform my faith and understanding? What challenges does it hold for me personally? Once certainty is destabilized, new questions, new depths of exploration and insight can be explored and a new integration of faith and life is required. To be willing to go beyond our comfort zone, to step over the threshold of certainty and find the capacity to live with uncertainty and not knowing paradoxically heralds the beginning of new insight: that is to say, living with uncertainty also entails living in faith.

Through these encounters the practitioners were brought to an awareness of the centrality to their personal and professional identity of living in faith: not seeing how things will be but living in hope that through one's own faithful practice and willingness to take the risk of loving encounter, God's purposes are being worked out. This was spoken of in the group as 'the hiddenness of the processes at work', a perception that required the need to trust that God is present in every kind of human experience, in pain and darkness as well as in the light.

David eventually saw his role as 'being there' (a phrase that needs much unpacking) in solidarity with and for Darren, waiting and hoping that a new thing might emerge. Head teacher Pat had to recognize that she did not know how the informal fostering arrangement would work out in the end but, for now, it was working and her response was to support Jean in her caring. The encounter between Tom and Mark was also characterized by a sense of the hiddenness of the processes at work. At the first meeting with Mark, Tom had no real idea of what the relationship might mean for Tom or indeed for himself as a religious professional in the future. What mattered was attention to the demand of the present encounter. As it happened, this encounter established a relationship that Mark felt able to trust so that he could approach Tom again when he needed to. Reflection on these encounters resulted in the recognition that it is not ours to know what hidden processes are at work in a situation, but it is our concern to take time to reflect on our encounters with others in an attempt to ensure that we remain, as far as possible, faithful practitioners.

The mature capacity to tolerate not knowing without the need to grasp after facts and certainty – what the poet Keats termed 'negative capability' – is characteristic of both the life of faith and of all creative endeavour. It is what the group characterized as 'practical mysticism': seeking to dwell in God while paying full attention to the present moment of encounter. The rest is not ours to know.

Emerging themes in organizations

Having heard the accounts from those crossing the boundaries between the organizational world and the Church, the next stage in the process was to identify themes and issues that arose and to see which questions were worth pursuing. This is inevitably a more expansive and discursive exercise that resists attempts to produce anything too systematic – at least, that was the experience of this particular group. It was interesting that the group contained a number of individuals who were familiar with acting in a consultancy capacity and that the various techniques employed in this profession then came to the fore in the subsequent discussions. It has to be said that the group found itself going in its own direction at this point rather than addressing the questions set in the conference, but that reflected the diversity of the material that was emerging and the range of experiences of the participants. The challenge was to find a way of organizing the ideas that were stimulated by the accounts and this became a more random process than had been anticipated.

THEME 1: Practices as life-affirming or life-denying

Aware of this, there was an attempt to produce a matrix on which it was possible to place both the accounts and the issues flowing from them in order to see if any clear pattern began to emerge. The two axes on this matrix were chosen because they seemed to reflect two of the major themes which ran through the discussions. The first was that of how humanizing or dehumanizing any particular account appeared to be, and the second was the extent to which each appeared to represent our understanding of the kingdom of God. This was inevitably somewhat subjective, but it offered a means of locating the experiences and deciding how they might be evaluated. Another theme that began to emerge was that of risk, and the extent to which the people involved in the situations being explored were prepared to 'go out on a limb' in order to pursue their chosen path. All of this makes this particular session rather difficult to convey with any degree of accuracy, so that needs to be borne in mind at this point.

The first axis, that of whether a specific example was humanizing or dehumanizing certainly demands considerable exploration. The group tended to operate with an intuitive understanding of what this meant rather than searching for definitive explanations. Other ways of describing this such as whether a particular practice was life-affirming or life-denying were also employed, but we acknowledged the complexity of this issue and the possibility of different judgements on such matters. We felt it was possible, in most cases, to see fairly clearly when humans and their relationships were being damaged or compromised in the examples under discussion.

In the first account then, that of the use of email in business organizations, the concern was that the extent of messages being sent and received, plus the expectations that now accompany this, that is that people would always be 'on call' and expected to respond as rapidly as possible, were indeed damaging to individuals involved. This seems to be a practice confined to the higher echelons of the commercial world though, and was not something experienced in quite the same way within church circles. This then led naturally into a further underlying debate about when and whether practice in the Church was somehow better or different from the rest of the organizational world. To what extent are churches – and that of course begs the question as to whether we mean the local church, the wider church, or even the various church hierarchies – to be understood as organizations, and, if so, how do they differ from secular organizations? This again, became another underlying theme that entered the discussions, but that we did not try to resolve at this point.

We did reach the conclusion that there is a clear danger in this type of discussion of demonizing the secular and romanticizing the religious, as if the former had always got it wrong and would be placed in the unfavourable section of the matrix, and that the religious tended to get it right. Given that employees from both sides of the boundary were present, we tried to take great care in being objective in our judgements rather than resorting to the easy caricatures known within each profession and becoming 'grumpy old men and women' complaining about obvious sources of dissatisfaction. What needed to be identified were examples of both good and bad practice from both sides of the boundary rather than simply praising one and damning the other.

This did make comparisons difficult at times, as for instance with the respective experiences of email. Not many clergy – unless perhaps they are senior bishops or diocesan officials – will encounter the level of demands reported from within the commercial world. Most parish clergy now certainly use email increasingly in dealing with matters such as checking draft wedding services or even funeral addresses, but this is seen as a useful process as part of a pastoral relationship, especially given that many weddings are dealt with at a distance rather than with couples who reside in a locality. But there was certainly concern that email messages received from the hierarchy could be difficult to interpret and required careful and considered response. One issue commonly raised is that of the danger of the rapid response rather than the more considered one that was previously involved in sitting down and composing a letter and in some cases, giving oneself time to calm down! Messages sent hurriedly because one is under pressure with many other emails to deal with, are seen as particularly vulnerable to misinterpretation and ill-considered responses.

This led into a discussion about the whole medium of electronic communication and both its advantages and disadvantages. The first seem reasonably obvious – when the system works well – rapid contact over time and distance, but with the recipient supposedly in control of when and how they respond. Within a pressured work context, however, this control is more limited because of the expectations that now accompany most communications. The key question appears to be of what the mode of communication does to human relationships and of how and when it enhances 'genuine' or authentic human contact – and there is an issue that needs exploring also – and when it reinforces relationships of power or dependency that one might want to express concerns about. It was noted that it is easy to say that email is itself neutral – neither good nor bad in itself – but that everything depends upon how it is being used in a specific content. But this is perhaps too simplistic as the system makes certain assumptions about how humans communicate and what is important in relationships. The lack of face-to-face contact and therefore the impossibility of interpreting body language as well as words is a major limitation of the system, although the introduction of video conferencing and skype of course does allow for some access to the body language of the other person. But there was a feeling that if communication is reduced to a written text on a screen, so does not even contain the tone of voice present in a phone call, then something important in human contact is in danger of being lost.

So there was a provisional conclusion that email in a high-pressured organizational setting, could indeed be dehumanizing and therefore also be working against the kingdom of God. Certainly if seen as a substitute for direct human encounter and a means simply of manipulating or reinforcing existing power relationships, then it is open to question. If, on the other hand, it is used as a supplement to an existing and well-established relationship, and simply a means of conveying information, then it can be a positive and indeed enhancing aspect of human communication. We were aware that there are other debates in this area about social networking sites and their potential for abuse, but this went beyond the scope of our discussions.

THEME 2: How do we value work?

Then there is clearly a much wider debate about the role of work itself in people's lives and when and under what conditions work is life-enhancing or life-denying. For the sake of argument, we tended to take work as meaning full-time paid employment, but were aware that this is a limited definition. Once again we wanted to be wary of any swift caricature of any specific organization or profession that fell into the trap of anecdotal complaints. We all grumble about our jobs and colleagues from time to time, but this is not the same as claiming that there is something inherently damaging about the nature of the work itself.

We acknowledged that, for many of us, work is a positive and often life-enhancing experience. Having a clear role, being able to develop one's abilities, the capacity to relate to others and to experience job satisfaction, let alone one's earning capacity and the possibility of providing for oneself and others can all be means of building self-esteem and confidence. There are, however, many situations where these factors are not present, and where workplace bullying, exploitation and inappropriate power relationships, lack of control over one's own time and subsequent impact upon personal and family life, are closer to the truth. Particularly in the current economic climate where there is both the fear and reality of job cuts in both public and private sectors, and the looming shadow of higher unemployment, there are massive pressures on people to take wage cuts or to work longer hours in order to remain in work. One could argue that the dangers of dehumanizing practices in the work setting are considerably heightened in this context. How one evaluates this from a kingdom perspective is clearly a major theological and ethical issue which should be explored to greater depth, and by using access to the resources of other disciplines.

THEME 3: Are religious organizations different from others?

Thus, the discussions moved into consideration of management styles and how secular and church organizations differed.

Are there ways in which humans can be treated with concern and respect even when circumstances are as difficult as they are currently and managers find themselves under significant pressures? It is obvious that some managers continue to behave with integrity and appropriate pastoral care whatever the situation, probably because they share the values of respect and care for others that might or might not come from a religious base. Having to make people redundant is a major test of how to handle difficult and painful situations, for instance, and this is where industrial chaplains can sometimes stand alongside the individuals on both sides and offer both practical and pastoral support. But how do those of faith who have to make the difficult decisions or to convey those to colleagues and workforce do so with integrity?

There is no shortage of examples of bad practice, where people are not treated with concern and respect, either where jobs are being lost, or where the pace of change is so rapid that human considerations appear to be abandoned. This emerged as a major theme within the group discussion. Implementing change – given that change is a permanent feature of many organizations – was identified as a real challenge. Quite often the processes employed appeared to be so task-oriented and target-driven, that the human beings caught up in this, their feelings, let alone their capacity to absorb rapid changes, were not taken into account. It was acknowledged that there are genuine tensions in this, that the organization is under its own pressures, sometimes for survival, and in order to protect jobs, and that it is not always possible to be as 'user friendly' as one would like. But it was also felt that the processes of change could be handled more effectively and efficiently if the human dimension was taken into account. Perhaps this is one area where the church-based experience of having to take people along with you might have something to say to the organizational world?

The focus of the discussions then shifted towards the religious organizations and how they fared according to the criteria. The tension between being 'caring' and trying to take into account feelings and strongly held views, and then the need for change and development, rapidly came to the surface. Those working more closely within the churches often experience their own frustrations that appropriate and timely change is very difficult to pursue. One of the factors is certainly that very often one is dealing with volunteers rather than employees, and that consensus and agreement is required before things can change, but one might also question whether it is accurate or helpful to think of the churches as organizations at all. Are the structures and protocols such that they bear comparison with secular organizations? There is much to be explored here, but we were aware that some of this work was happening within the theological world – are churches networks, associations, organizations or what?

What also came across strongly though was a feeling that the churches had failed to grasp the changed operating environment in which we now find ourselves. Those who regularly cross the boundary into the secular world report growing hostility, suspicion, questioning of motives and practice, and a general view that Christians are somehow 'odd and irrational' and to be kept at arm's length. This contrasts with the self-understanding, within the Church of England in particular, that it has an automatic and unquestioned right to be present in the wider society and should have a voice in public affairs. This is also an increasing experience of parish ministry it needs to be said, where ministers find themselves having to earn respect and to justify their presence beyond the life of their local congregations. This may be one reason why so many have abandoned crossing the boundaries at all and prefer to remain within 'the enclave of recognition' as W. H. Vanstone once described it. Another is lack of time and capacity of course. But for those who do cross those boundaries as a major part of their ministry, the challenge is to accept that their role and very presence cannot be taken for granted.

This is but one example of the churches' limited capacity to absorb and respond to change. Should others be sought, one would not have to look very far. Current debates about women bishops and homosexuality are other obvious examples where the churches appear to be obsessed with issues that the wider society has sorted out long ago and where they are seen as anachronistic and out of touch. These may not appear to impinge directly upon the presence of those of faith within the secular world, but they do have a very public impact upon perceptions and responses once one attempts to work outside the congregational enclave. One recalls debates from the 1980s about the rise of a church-centred more evangelical approach which risked turning churches into enclosed sects and wonders whether this is now the position that has been reached.

There are then further questions about internal church organizational practice in terms of working relationships and structures and whether there are not things to be learnt from the secular world about good practice. The experiences of front-line clergy certainly vary from diocese to diocese within the Church of England, and there are numerous examples of 'bad management' from the hierarchy. But are bishops and archdeacons supposed to be 'managers'? Parish clergy now in charge of increasing numbers of parishes are also finding themselves having to fulfil managerial functions for which they have not been trained or which are not consistent with their calling as they perceive it. The pace and nature of change within church structures has created a new and often disconcerting internal operating environment and little thought or preparation has been given to this. Hence there is a direct parallel with the secular experience of managers who have the challenge of implementing significant organizational change. There is role confusion and subsequent frustration at all levels of church life – lay people finding themselves taking over the previous roles of their clergy, looking after the fabric of their local churches, leading worship, exercising pastoral care etc. Much of this happens by default as much as by design and the feelings of those caught up in this process are very rarely recognized or taken into account.

This is the tip of the iceberg in terms of the actual discussions, but does offer some flavour of the emerging themes in this part of the conference. Whether one is talking about the Church or about secular organizations, a question that we kept returning to is that of whether it is the case that if human beings are treated with more concern and respect then the organization is more likely to be efficient and effective. There is evidence to suggest that this is often the case. Care for the people and one creates a far better working environment whatever the tasks. So if the value of human wellbeing is built into the organization, perhaps it stands a better chance of achieving its objectives, whatever they might be. Human flourishing as a core value emerges as a central theme of these discussions.

Emerging themes in communities

The sharing of encounters led to intensive discussions about what it meant to be an ordained minister or Christian practitioner in community settings. Were all marginalized communities the same? How does the minister or practitioner enter into that marginalization? Should energy be focused on structures or individuals or both? These questions seemed interrelated. A feeling of being on the same page, of having enough in common to engage at depth started to develop in the small group.

THEME 1: The way in which perception and identity shape each other both for communities and workers

In reflecting upon the encounters related in the previous chapter, the group became aware that the communities they worked in often had an identity that shaped the way they were perceived but then negative perceptions reinforced a community identity of powerlessness and inability to change. This reflection had its parallels in being a worker identified that such communities. On the one hand, there were the pressures to be the problem solver while at the same time experiencing the powerlessness of the residents. Pauline recounted the powerful feelings she had on agreeing to move into the community she served and the strength of the identities projected onto her by colleagues when they learned of her decision. By some she was regarded as foolhardy and unlikely to cope, by others she was ascribed an exaggerated saintliness that she would live in such a place. Before she even arrived she felt that her identity and that of the community were becoming intertwined.

For communities there was a sense that they lived up to their bad reputations. This not only applied to residents but also to service providers who had low expectations that they could deliver high-quality services in a way that met residents' needs. Luke observed the energy that had been put into deciding whose responsibility it was to respond to the suicidal woman rather than using that energy to supply the help she needed. The excessive attention to boundary work suggested low expectations of offering a high-quality service.

For residents there was the sense that there was a broader 'system' that set the agenda and which they were powerless to influence. This was particularly acute for communities that were affected by spatial segregation both in terms of social housing allocation and in terms of market decisions not to buy property in their area. Work done to improve the quality and physical attractiveness of social housing was appreciated but this in itself did not constitute a regenerated community, a more profound social regeneration was required in which a positive identity enabled opportunities to be identified and taken. Phillip felt that the positive image of the Housing Association was an important component in giving the communities it served a positive image. Reflecting the composition of those communities in the governance structures of the Association was at least as important as the physical condition of the housing stock.

Ministers resident in marginalized communities face particular dilemmas. They are often the only resident professional with other professionals driving into the community to teach, police, support housing etc. They thus have a blurred identity of being both resident and professional. Both the Church and other agencies expect them to play a key role in projects and initiatives designed to regenerate the community. There can be unrealistic expectations that they will have the answers to the complex issues of inter-agency working and residents with multiple and complex needs. A huge amount of their time may be spent 'humanizing' externally imposed initiatives in an attempt to make them relevant to the local context. This can lead to a sense of needing to 'fit in' other priestly work such as leading worship, offering the occasional offices and pastoral care for individuals. All these pressures can lead to a sense that their work and their community are their identity. The overwhelming nature of the work can then lead them to disengage from reflection, support and networking. Wider church structures are often just pleased to have someone willing to be resident in 'difficult' communities and so are wary of 'off-loading' by these ministers in case it indicates that all is not well. Ministers can also suffer from the guilt that they have the resources to 'escape' for holidays or days off when residents cannot. They also know they are resident until they choose to leave, a choice not available to most of their neighbours. Dealing with this outsider/insider identity presents many dilemmas. Should the primary focus of ministry be working with the structures that shape life in the community or with the individuals affected by those structures? Should external interventions 'for the benefit' of the community be shaped or resisted? What sort of risks is it appropriate to take both personally and with the reputation of the Church and what accountability structures support such risk taking? Will the price of 'success' be a move to yet another disempowered and marginalized community to begin again?

THEME 2: The difference between regenerating 'bland' and 'vibrant' communities

Through the dialogue of the action learning event we found two different experiences of working in the regeneration of communities. Those working in inner-city communities were dealing with the benefits and challenges of highly diverse communities, where people of different religions and ethnic groups lived side by side and where there was a mix of long-term residents and those who were making use of the cheap housing as a temporary home with the aspiration to move 'up and out'. Such communities faced the challenge of overstretched public services, poor-quality housing, high crime and the presence of drugs and prostitution. They often benefited from a good range of shops, small businesses providing work and faith communities willing to be in dialogue for the benefit of the neighbourhood. Effective regeneration work was often about getting people to talk and acknowledge that they had problems in common. Philip saw the Housing Association as an important site for such conversations enabling people with diverse backgrounds and expectations to cooperate because of a shared need for good housing. He felt his role as a Christian practitioner was to highlight the importance of how these conversations were conducted.

Those working in 'outer estates' or post-industrial towns faced a different set of challenges. They were working in predominantly white working-class communities with many families experiencing bad health and inter-generational work-lessness. Public services were often of low quality, struggling to recruit people to work in them and with low expectations of the population. The stigmatizing effect of living in these communities often thwarted attempts to gain an education or work. Nevertheless, these communities often housed extended families and so had a loyalty to the place that resented the idea that to 'move up' meant 'moving out'. The absence of shops, banks and employers in these communities sent out a message that they had lost their economic rationale and so at-tempting to find work would only meet with disappointment. Many of these communities had had considerable sums spent on physical regeneration, improving the quality of housing and creating amenities such as open spaces. However, what was required in addition was social and economic regenera-tion giving a sense of worth and purpose to the community. Pauline found the idea of social capital helpful in exploring her context. There were powerful networks of relationships be-tween extended families that provided bonding social capital and a sense of loyalty to the community itself. However, this was insufficient without bridging social capital that brought residents into contact with each other across the community – she felt the choir achieved this. What was also needed was linking social capital communicating the real needs of the community to those in power. Pauline's status as a profes-sional but also a resident made her key in linking social capital and generated pressures for her to adopt a pivotal role in the community.

The experience of living and working in these communities for ministers could be very different. In the vibrant communities it was possible to capture something of the excitement of constant change and the task of building relationships, although intense, could be very satisfying. In the bland communities it was common to experience something of the abandonment felt by the residents and to struggle to get participation in regeneration projects. The skills of reading and interpreting context were crucial to working effectively with communities, yet there was little training available particularly to ministers to learn this skill, whether formally or through coaching on the job.

THEME 3: Working with or against the system that frames the life of the community

For those working in communities, each day can feel like a series of ethical dilemmas as to whether they should be working with or against the system that frames the life of the community. Faced with a person in crisis, the instinct is to act as their advocate in obtaining the support they need from the system as it is. Certainly Luke and Kirsty felt they had to adopt this role. Pressure of work often does not allow time to go back and challenge the system and there can be difficulties in making a complaint on behalf of someone who is under too much pressure to make a complaint themselves. More effective can be membership of partnerships, project boards and local forums that do have a voice on local service delivery. However, time spent in such meetings is time not spent with community members, which in itself creates dilemmas. Ministers are often school governors or even chairs of school governing bodies and well aware that this is time-consuming and exacting work, needing the mastery of large amounts of technical detail rather than time spent building relationships with parents and children. Pauline struggled with the feeling that she was 'fitting in' pastoral work around the meetings that structured her diary.

Having decided what balance of time should be spent with individual community members as opposed to the structures that frame the life of the community, a further dilemma arises about the approach to be taken. Should the focus be on advocacy for individuals so they get the services they need? Should the focus be on working with structures for incremental reform by being in sympathy and solidarity with those seeking to serve the community who themselves are often struggling with external pressures such as government policy and funding. Should the focus be on working in an oppositional way, mobilizing discontent and making demands rather than negotiating? The Christian tradition has advocates of all three approaches. To some extent the approach may be dictated by the role the person has in the community. A chair of a school governing body would find it difficult to take an oppositional approach to government education policy without the support of the head teacher given the reputational costs for the school. For priests and ministers the dilemma is often whether to take an approach with which members of their church would find uncomfortable.

A further ethical issue is to retain an appropriate sense of where individual responsibility lies. In communities whose members face genuine difficulties, some of which are exacerbated by poor-quality housing, poor-quality services and lack of work opportunities, it can be difficult to know what expectations to place on community members to act in their own self-interest. On the one hand, there can be the danger of infantilizing and expecting nothing, on the other hand lies the danger of expecting residents to draw on reserves of social capital which they do not possess. There are some problems, such as addictions and mental health issues, which impair the capacity of an individual to make decisions in their own best interests. How are such people to be supported? This issue is particularly pertinent in a political climate that seeks to place more responsibility on individuals to be self-reliant, economically active and taking advantage of support that will lessen their dependency on the state.

For these practitioners, working in communities inevitably had a political dimension. Having space to identify the political challenges and develop responses was seen as something theological reflection could help with.

Concluding commentary

By the end of this phase in the event, participants were energized by the feeling that they could identify significant issues which they felt they shared. When the three groups fed back to each other there was a sense that the issues from other groups made sense within the conversation about pastoral practice and public theology. The sense that church based ministers on the one hand and institutionally based chaplains, professionals and managers on the other were from different worlds was dissolving. There was confidence that a shared agenda was emerging and anticipation that the next step of turning to the Christian tradition would be worthwhile.

5

Engaging with Scripture

Introductory commentary

This chapter describes that part of the pastoral cycle that turns to the Christian tradition for insights. This is not to assume that the Christian tradition has so far been absent from the conversation. It has shaped those who take part and influences what is selected for discussion and the tone of that discussion. In the action learning event upon which the book is based it was decided to turn to scripture at this point in the pastoral cycle because it was assumed this would be a shared text that would allow participants from different traditions to work together in a process of discernment. Professor Christopher Rowland, Dean Ireland Professor of Biblical Exegesis at the University of Oxford, kindly offered to support this part of the process. He listened to the issues that had emerged from exploring the encounters and proposed a thematic approach to using the Bible and three themes we could use to inform our reflections.

One of the values of experiential learning events is the opportunity to learn the unexpected. Our expectation that participants would readily turn to the Bible as a shared text proved faulty. A number of concerns about using the Bible were raised. This chapter has two concluding commentaries which seek to set out and address those concerns. The first is by the authors and offers their interpretation of the difficulties that arose. The second commentary is by Chris Rowland and offers insights and critique from his commitment to contextual approaches (Bennett and Rowland, 2005).

How to engage? A thematic approach

The pastoral cycle assumes that experience is the starting point for the group coming together to reflect theologically. It identifies a shared interest that animates the discussion and a shared commitment to the Christian tradition that makes a turn to that tradition an essential element in the process. This approach is particularly favoured by the liberation theologies that start with the shared concerns of particular groups such as the poor, women, indigenous people or marginalized ethnic groups.

Chris Rowland shared with the group his experiences of working alongside theologians and church communities in Latin America. He described the way in which they had used the pastoral cycle and the Bible to gain insights into their situation and to decide upon actions to improve it.

The approach to scripture that was suggested was to use broad themes to get a sense of the overall meaning of scripture and then use those themes to help interpret particular passages. The thematic approach argues that there is an overall coherence to the Bible as the site of God's self-revelation. Even though the Bible is a collection of books by different authors, of different genres, written at different times and places and in different languages, it nevertheless offers an account of God that is consistent. The gift brought to the group by Chris Rowland was the sense of the relationship between the whole and the parts. This approach was empowering for the group who were more accustomed to reading small passages of scripture prescribed by the lectionary rather than thinking about whole books and the themes that run across the whole of scripture.

As the three themes were presented there was a sense of recognition that they had something to say to the struggle for human flourishing that was emerging in the event.

The next three sections sketch in the themes, offering Bible passages that illustrate them. Quotations are from the New Revised Standard Version of the Bible.

THEME A: The breaking in of the kingdom

With the coming of Christ a new age has decisively broken in. We are invited to experience life in all its fullness. We are called to act as if it is already real while being aware that it is not yet fully realized. This enables us to hold hope and reality in tension.

Jesus' sermon at the synagogue in Nazareth sees him announcing the year of the Lord, a decisive turn in history.

> He stood up to read, and the scroll of the prophet Isaiah was given to him. He unrolled the scroll and found the place where it was written:
> 'The Spirit of the Lord is upon me, because he has anointed me to bring good news to the poor.
> He has sent me to proclaim release to the captives and recovery of sight to the blind,
> To let the oppressed go free, to proclaim the year of the Lord's favour.'
> And he rolled up the scroll, gave it back to the attendant, and sat down. The eyes of all in the synagogue were fixed on him. Then he began to say to them, 'Today this scripture has been fulfilled in your hearing.' (Luke 4.16–21)

Central to the Christian hope for human flourishing is the struggle to taste heaven on earth. This is exemplified in the Lord's Prayer:

Pray then in this way:
'Our Father in Heaven, hallowed be your name.
Your kingdom come.
Your will be done on earth as it is in heaven.
Give us this day our daily bread.
And forgive us our debts, as we also have forgiven our
debtors.
And do not bring us to the time of trial, but rescue us from
the evil one.'
(Matthew 6.9–13)

The priorities of the kingdom of heaven turn out to be different from what people are expecting. Justice seems to be related to needs rather than deserts and status comes through service rather than position. Matthew 20 contains two illustrative stories. The first (Matthew 20.1–16) is a parable in which a landowner hires day labourers to work in his vineyard at an agreed daily rate. He returns to the market and recruits further labourers during the course of the day. At the end of the day he pays each person the same amount. Those who have 'borne the burden of the day and the scorching heat' complain that they have been badly treated. The employer asserts his right to be generous. The parable concludes, 'The last will be first and the first will be last' (Matthew 20.16).

The second is an account of a conversation between Jesus and the mother of two of his disciples. In response to Mrs Zebedee's request that her sons sit at the right and left hand of Jesus when he comes into his kingdom, Jesus reasserts the priorities of the kingdom.

'You know that the rulers of the Gentiles lord it over them and their great ones are tyrants over them. It will not be so among you; but whoever wishes to be great among you must be your servant, and whoever wishes to be first among

77

you must be your slave; just as the Son of Man came not to be served but to serve, and to give his life a ransom for many.' (Matthew 20.25–8 NRSV)

The confidence to enact the kingdom while accepting that all is not as we would wish is central to Christian hope. The kingdom is already inaugurated by Christ's life, death and resurrection but it is yet to be fully realized. Wheat and weeds continue to grow together (Matthew 13.24–30).

THEME B: Christ's love crosses boundaries

Those on the edge are now in the centre, for example, the child, the untouchable leper, and the possessed. The Church exemplifies a community of equals in which our differences are a source of strength albeit problematic at times. The governing principle is love.

The Gospels are full of stories that show Christ crossing boundaries of social acceptability. These stories have given Christians a special concern for the marginalized. From the encounters that participants brought to the event came a sense of not only wanting to cross boundaries but being aware that they are also part of the structures that can create those boundaries in the first place.

Jesus presents the child as an exemplar of the kingdom.

Whoever becomes humble like this child is the greatest in the kingdom of heaven.
Whoever welcomes one such child in my name welcomes me. (Matthew 18.4–5)

In the story of the Canaanite woman (Matthew 15.21–6) Jesus suggests to the woman that his ministry is only to the house of Israel. She replies, 'Yes Lord, yet even the dogs eat the crumbs that fall from their masters' table' (v. 27). By acknowledging her excluded status as a non-Jew the woman pushes for inclusion in the banquet of the kingdom. Jesus commends her and grants her request.

It is sometimes possible to ascribe a concern with inclusion/exclusion symbolized by cleanliness as a preoccupation of less sophisticated societies than our own. Yet the encounters described in Chapter 3 show societal roles and systems seeking to 'sort' people into their proper place. There remain boundaries to be crossed.

> A leper came to him begging him, and kneeling he said to him, 'If you choose, you can make me clean.' Moved with pity, Jesus stretched out his hand and touched him, and said to him, 'I do choose. Be made clean!' (Mark 1.40–2)

In these Gospel passages we can see a struggle to bring what is marginalized to the centre of attention – a struggle that can also be recognized in the blurred encounters recorded in this book.

Paul helps the Corinthians (see 1 Corinthians 12 and 13) understand their incorporation into Christ and so their responsibility as members. He urges them to overcome their divisions by seeing love as the power that unifies and animates the body. He acknowledges the limitations of our current knowledge of God but promises a fulfilment of God's love.

> For now we see in a mirror dimly, but then we will see face to face. Now I know only in part; then I will know fully, even as I have been fully known. And now faith, hope, and love abide, these three; and the greatest of these is love. (1 Corinthians 13.12–13)

Bringing the language of love to the secular situations described in this book provokes tensions that are picked up in Chapter 6.

THEME C: Unmasking the Empire

The principalities and powers, economic and political, can be unmasked for what they are. They may hold sway now but in the end evil will be defeated. A key challenge in the encounters offered in this book is naming that which is antagonistic to human flourishing. In a desire to get the best out of the system for those we are seeking to help, it is easier not to name the political and economic realities we encounter.

The strand of apocalyptic literature in the Bible uses highly symbolic language to do that naming. It is as if the imagery sets the writers free to tell it as it is. They describe vividly that which seeks to overcome good and long for its downfall. The writer of Revelation is thought to have been wrestling with the evils of the Roman Empire whose power seemed so total and unassailable. This book is not written in a situation of political terror or totalitarianism but it is written at a time of shifting foundations when people struggle to name what is good and what is bad in the systems that shape their lives. The civil unrest of August 2011, set alongside the misuse of power by media, politicians and the financial sector, have led for some to a sense that the love of mammon has an unshakeable grip on society.

In amazement the whole earth followed the beast. They worshipped the dragon, for he had given his authority to the beast, and they worshipped the beast, saying, 'Who is like the beast and who can fight against it.' (Revelation 13.3–4)

These are united in yielding their power and authority to the beast; they will make war on the Lamb, and the Lamb will conquer them, for he is Lord of lords and King of kings, and those with him are called and chosen and faithful. (Revelation 17.13–14)

At such times it is difficult to feel that an agenda that puts 'the least of these' in the centre will triumph. This theme advocates an unmasking and naming of the 'principalities and powers' in the confidence that righteousness will reign.

These three themes informed the discussion that is presented in Chapter 6. But before turning to that it is important to explore the problems the group faced in engaging with scripture. It is unlikely that they will be the only group to have such problems, and it is hoped that a discussion of them here will assist readers in their own theological reflection.

Concluding commentary 1: Problems of engaging

On reflection, the difficulties in turning to scripture might have been anticipated. In teaching the pastoral cycle to ministerial students it is a frequent experience that they enjoy describing and analysing an issue but then want to jump to planning for the future without engaging with the Christian tradition. The experienced practitioners taking part in the event raised issues that helped illuminate the problem of engaging with scripture.

A useful model for discussing hermeneutics, the interpretation of scripture, is to identify three locations from which that interpretation might take place. One is 'behind the text', that is exploring the world of the author, to examine issues such as who the book was written by, its intended audience, the historical context, the geographical setting and the purpose of the book. Another is 'within the text' examining such concerns as the original language of the book, its genre, its structure and use of literary devices. The final location is 'in front of the text' focusing on the perspectives and concerns which the reader brings to the text (H+ Making Good Sense of the Bible, 2011).

The problems the participants found can be grouped into three categories. Concerns about their expertise in the world of the author, doubts about whether their concerns as readers could be brought to the text and a reticence in making use of scripture in the contexts in which they worked. Each of these is addressed in turn.

Getting stuck behind the text

There was a sense from a number of participants that the Bible was for experts. As ordinary Christian practitioners they could not be expected to have the necessary knowledge and skill to use scripture in theological reflection.

Miroslav Volf argues that in the 1960s a major shift occurred with leading theologians no longer engaging directly with the biblical text. Biblical scholars focused on the world behind the text and concentrated on historical approaches to the text. Volf summarizes the impact of this thus:

> A wide chasm opened between the work of systematic theologians and biblical scholars: systematic theologians abandoned the Bible to biblical scholars-turned-historians, and biblical scholars offloaded theology onto systematic theologians. The result? Locked into a distant past, the Bible became lost to the present, as far as academic theology was concerned. (Volf, 2010, pp. 8–9)

More recently a post-liberal approach to biblical interpretation has emerged which Walter Brueggemann describes as having a number of characteristics. First, it has revalued the imagination working alongside reason in interpreting the text. Next it accepts that all readings come from somewhere, and so the ideological concerns of the reader can be brought under scrutiny. All readers have a context which shapes their reading. Finally, such readings have an urgency that arises from the needs of the community in which they take place. (Brueggemann, 2005, p. 170)

John Barton argues for the on-going importance of biblical criticism:

> Most people go to the Bible because they think it will illuminate human life, and biblical criticism has no vested interest in denying this. What it does set up is a procedural distinction between discovering what the texts mean and evaluating or using them. . . It must be possible to establish what the text means, regardless of one's own convictions. If they turn out to support those convictions that is a great gain; whereas if one takes the convictions as part of one's presuppositions in reading the text, there is always the danger of simply seeing one's own face at the bottom of the well. (Barton, 2007, p. 188)

Barton expresses a desire not to lose the scholarship about what lies behind the text in the new enthusiasm for re-engaging with the Bible as a text relevant to practice. These trends in biblical scholarship and theology have influenced the way in which each generation has been prepared for ministry in the Church. There has been a substantial period in which ministerial training has emphasized knowledge about the world of the author – behind the text. This has generated anxieties about being seen to use the Bible in an unsophisticated way and so largely confined the Bible to preaching. There are anxieties about offering an interpretation of a text in front of other theologically trained people in case that interpretation is exposed as naïve.

Having honest doubts in front of the text

For those working in secular settings engaging mainly with those who have no faith and who have had little or no contact with the Christian tradition, there were doubts about the relevance of the Bible. It is not just that the Bible has lost salience but also that any sense of referring to an external tradition in guiding action seems alien. If there was a point of contact it was found in using the language of spirituality but the reference point for that spirituality was the self and a subjective world view rather than any external transcendent reference point or sense of objective truth to which the self should conform. This is the picture painted in *The Spiritual Revolution* by Heelas and Woodward (2005), who distinguish between the 'life-as' spirituality of traditional congregations and the 'subjective-life' spirituality of New Age practices. Their definitions of the two types show that tradition plays a part in the first but not the second.

> Life-as forms of the sacred, which emphasize a transcendent source of significance and authority to which individuals must conform at the expense of the cultivation of their unique subject-lives.
> Subjective-life forms of the sacred, which emphasize inner sources of significance and authority and the cultivation or sacralization of unique subjective-lives. (p. 6)

Of course subjective-life spiritualities are likely to draw upon external resources in the process of sacralization but they do not necessarily accord those sources authority. For practitioners working with people whose world view does not include an authoritative tradition, referring to sacred texts may in itself be confusing. Some of these practitioners have tapped into the skills of cultural interpretation possessed by their clients and used cultural resources such as film, music and novels to spark conversations about meaning and purpose (Lynch, 2005).

A closely related concern was that to turn to the Bible is to turn away from the world and its concerns. The privatization of Christianity means that worship and the private devotional reading by Christians are now seen as the key contexts in

which the Bible is read. To make use of the Bible in reflecting on secular settings is to turn away from the reality of the
context and to return to the internal concerns of the Church.
For authorized ministers working in secular settings there is
an awareness of the way in which the Church can pull all
discussions towards its own preoccupations of internal order
and away from the realities of mission.

For those practitioners dealing with marginalized groups
there was a suspicion of the Bible as a text that has been
abused to oppress women and minorities. Depictions of the
God of the Bible as misogynist, homophobic and racist are
present in the popular literature of the new atheists. That
some practices of some churches fall short of socially accepted
norms of equality and inclusion is evident and frequently represented in the media. An attempt to represent God as loving
and inclusive was not felt to be assisted by the 'texts of terror'
found within the books of the Bible (Trible, 1984).

These honest doubts were calmed by the idea that the
over-riding themes of the Bible could be used as hermeneutic
keys in interrogating difficult passages but they were not
completely overcome.

Reticence in sharing the text

For some practitioners, a liberal theology and years of living
with honest doubts had resulted in a habitual reticence about
the Bible which it was difficult to articulate or reverse. Being
accustomed to working in plural settings, their emphasis was
on listening to the stories of others and showing respect for
people of other faith traditions. For some, the settings in which
they worked placed a strong emphasis on respecting diversity and seeking inclusion and that had led to a self-censoring
of faith language. The emphasis was on presence rather than
engagement in faith dialogue.

This did not mean that the Bible was not a significant or formative text for them as religious practitioners. Many were committed to patterns of private prayer and public liturgy that drew extensively on the Bible through lectionary readings. The sense was that the work of the Bible was forming them as people of faith so that they were equipped and sustained in their mission in the world.

Finally, there was a reticence in turning to a text that is more than a classic of the English language but when viewed as scripture makes claims upon its readers. Volf describes the nature of scripture as follows:

> For others to insert us into their story and envision the proper end of our lives, define for us the source and substance of human flourishing, and tell us what we should or should not desire, is for them to violate us as self-standing individuals. The Bible as a sacred text, however, does just that. (Volf, 2010, p. 33)

Closely accompanying a pluralism that is dominated by secular voices rather than those shaped by faith, can be a relativism that resists any external referents when defining human flourishing. Phrases such as 'What works for you' or 'Whatever floats your boat' suggest that respect for the other comes from allowing people to define their individual view of human flourishing rather than engaging in dialogue to seek a collective view. The very thought of a collective idea of the good society is resisted by an unreflective relativism but the reality is that this is the milieu in which many practitioners operate. Pastoral experience had led some participants to give up the possibility of a public theology. It is the hope of the authors that engaging in theological reflection will also lead to a recovery of confidence in public theology. The next chapter offers some tentative contributions to that public theology.

Concluding commentary 2: Reflections from Chris Rowland

The situation we experienced at the action learning event reflects problems with the Bible and its role, which have a long history. Liberation theology put back two things on the interpretative agenda: first, the priority of real, everyday, life of one engaging with the Bible, wherever that is experienced; and, as a result, encouraging an imaginative engagement with the Bible in which the latter was illuminated by the questions put to it by life. There is an entirely understandable unease about the view that we can have access to 'what the Bible *really* says'. William Blake knew the Bible better than any historical critic but could see the Bible's many shortcomings as well as its strengths. He rejected the notion that any sacred text, without the input of interpreters and their experience, can define for us its true meaning and its impact on our lives. So, we should not deny the way in which our experience is the motor of our biblical interpretation, whoever, and wherever, we are.

One of the perennial problems that confront the practitioner is the disjuncture between the committed involvement in the project and the relationship to the Bible and the Christian tradition. What happened at the action-learning event exemplified this. The issue discussed in this chapter is as much, if not more, the nature of the process rather than the content of what was said, though that *was* an attempt to tailor to the perceived needs of the participants, at least in general terms, if not in particular.

Given the chronic nature of the problem that practitioners have struggling to make connections with the Bible, we attempted to set up a process which sought to take seriously this problem and bring the issue to the surface. Practitioners who are doing their work from a conviction that is rooted in the Christian tradition need to learn that one has to put as much effort into the biblical hermeneutics as into the reflection on practice. There is no easy route from the contemporary context to the Bible, and perhaps even after much patient struggle the way will be found to be completely closed off. In the action-learning event we tried to model a 'blurred encounter', a way of dealing with this, albeit in a necessarily truncated form. We did this by Helen communicating with Chris a couple of hours in advance of his sessions what their major issues were thus giving some adequate notice and allowing him to put together a response. That above all else was signalling that the Bible is turned to at a secondary stage, to assist with reflection, and that the role of both Bible and expert is to help with reflections on the issues that the particular contextual engagement throws up. Practitioners have to disabuse themselves of the fact that there is some magic hermeneutical formula out there which will help. What any Christian has to face up to is whether and how one engages with the Bible and, if one does, what is going to contribute to rather than inhibit reflection. If the Bible is not working as a stimulus then one might have to look elsewhere and be up front about facing up to that. Of course, one has to face up to the issue of why we should have recourse to the Bible *at all* if there is any resistance or doubt. There may be a temptation to think that if only we submit ourselves to the Bible all will be well, and that it is all a problem of liberal theology. But if liberal theology has done anything it has been to remind us that the Bible never speaks to our context directly. There is also a temptation to make a distinction between 'what the texts mean and evaluating or using them', a point made by many biblical historical critics. The problem with this is that in the light of Gadamer's work we can no longer think that *any* interpretation is free of cultural prejudice (Gadamer, 2004). We have to face up to the fact that we must recognize that we are all contextual theologians now.

What drew the participants in the event together was the fact that they all recognized that they were involved in situations that moved across their professional boundaries. That issue is at the heart of any contemporary theological reflection. What is necessary is to find a way of getting the practitioners to articulate what it is about their faith commitment that drew them to their work and which aspects of it continue to undergird and inspire it. In a more leisurely environment, helping practitioners to articulate for themselves what it is about their Christian (or indeed any other religious) commitment that makes them tick is crucial. Once that is done, and one has mapped the terrain across the boundary with the particular context one can look for ways across from one to the other. That normally has to be done one to one. At the event the boundary crossing was done between a corporate experience of both commitment and social analysis. All had this in common, namely, that the theological, however each defined it, was crucial as a motivating factor. Teasing this out is important. Once that is done – and it *has* to be done on an individual basis, some assistance can be given by the biblical expert, *ad personam,* to find ways of relating that which each thinks is the power of the faith commitment and gospel agenda which pushes them to make connections between it and their professional situation. That is never easy, nor can the personal task be short-circuited. The danger is offering generalities, which do not address the particulars of a situation.

So, what practitioners need who want to have recourse to the Bible is something more 'bespoke', which takes account of the particularities of their situation. That means sitting down with a sympathetic theologian with hermeneutical awareness of the problems and the opportunities of such boundary crossing and seeking to negotiate a route, exploring the struggle to relate Bible and life, and facing up to the fact that the Bible may be a hindrance rather than a help, before moving painfully towards a solution, if such there is. The important issue is that no writer, past or present, offers an easy answer but points us to the exercise of our interpretative imaginations.

This point is crucial. One of the issues around a corporate learning event such as the one that took place at Cuddesdon is that Chris responded to what emerged from a group which had formed at the event, which had come together because of general concerns but had different experiences and needs. In other words, the issues that emerged and which were engaged with were not *immediately* those of the individuals in their work contexts so much as that which had emerged as a result of the new context. In such corporate learning contexts what is necessary is that participants have to translate what is learnt in the new context to that which is the case outside the group in their day-to-day work. It is grasping less the details of what was said in terms of the theological content and more the process that was modelled. It is the process of reflection rather than content that would be universally applicable.

The issue of the relationship of contemporary situations with the Bible is one that has been wrestled with by Latin American liberation theologians. Their context is different. This was one of the pieces of input at the session on the Bible during the event. The challenge is more to persuade people to see the Bible as a collection which may speak to life outside the life of the Church. Clodovis Boff (Boff, 1987; and Sugirtharajah, 1991, pp. 9–35) describes two different kinds of approach to the Bible. One is more immediate, in which the biblical story becomes a type for the people of God in the modern world. The first of these Boff calls 'correspondence of terms'.

Correspondence of Terms:
Clodovis Boff *Theology and Praxis*

$$\frac{\text{scripture}}{\text{its political context}} = \frac{\text{theology of the political}}{\text{our political context}}$$

Here a reader identifies with a person or event in the Bible and sees the biblical situation being re-enacted in the modern. It involves insertion of oneself and one's life experiences into the biblical narrative so that the Bible offers a way of speaking directly about and indeed understanding, for example, displacement and homelessness, being an oppressed people. Thus, the biblical stories are seen to reflect *directly* and indeed unproblematically on the experiences of displacement, poverty and powerlessness. The correspondence of terms has many similarities with the kind of interpretation we find in a passage such as 1 Corinthians 10.11, where Paul tells the Corinthians that what was written in the Bible was directed to *them* in particular: 'These things happened to them to serve as an example, and they were written down to instruct us, on whom the ends of the ages have come.' Like Paul's addressees, the peasants of Latin America no more thought of their struggle for life and health in biblical terms every moment but, in the process of reflecting, the Bible functioned as a typological resource which gave meaning and hope.

In this kind of engagement with the Bible, the words become the catalyst for discernment of the divine way in the present. So, there is a corresponding emphasis on the Spirit rather than on the literal interpretation of texts, and this is accompanied by the conviction that the indwelling Spirit qualified the writer or speaker to 'bring the divine down to earth' in an arresting, authoritative way. In this kind of hermeneutic the words of the Bible become less an authoritative guide to life than a gateway to communion with the Divine Word through the Spirit, and that communion enables new types of understanding which are socially and contextually meaningful.

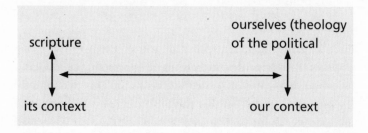

scripture

ourselves (theology of the political

its context

our context

The other model Boff entitles 'correspondence of relationships'. Here the Bible is read through the lens of the experience of the present, thereby enabling it to become a key to understanding that to which the scriptural text bears witness with regard to the life and struggles of the ancestors in the faith. This exploration of scripture in turn casts light on the present. In other words, the Bible is not itself the pattern but is more of an analogy in which the dialectical relationship between what happened then, or what is described in the pages of the Bible is seen as reflecting the life of the people of God at a particular time and place, the understanding and application of which is illuminated by the present struggles of the people of God. The Bible does not offer teaching so much as inspiration.

What is important about Boff's model is that it is not a quest for formulas to 'copy' or techniques to 'apply' from scripture. Through the model, scripture offers orientations, models, types, directives, principles, and inspirations – elements permitting us to acquire, on our own initiative, a 'hermeneutic competency'. This then offers the capacity to judge – for ourselves, in our own right – 'according to the mind of

Christ', or 'according to the Spirit', the new unpredictable situations with which we are continually confronted. The Christian writings offer us not a *what*, but a *how* – a manner, a style, a spirit (Sugirtharajah, 1991, p. 30).

Conclusion

This chapter has sought to engage with scripture. The hermeneutic approach adopted has been outlined and three themes have been set out for further reflection. The themes from this chapter are taken forward into the last part of the pastoral cycle described in Chapter 6 in which the learning from the encounters is expressed as a series of solidarities and tensions which are offered as a tentative contribution from pastoral practice to public theology. However, the chapter has also tried to be honest about the difficulties participants expressed about this part of the process and to suggest explanations for them. The first concluding commentary gave the authors' reactions. The second concluding commentary offered Chris Rowland's reflections.

6

Learning from the Encounters

Introductory commentary

The usual outcome of the pastoral cycle is that participants seek to change their practice or what they believe about their practice. This is highly contextual and specific to the time and situation of the reflectors. The action learning event underpinning this book invited people to work in small groups and to end the cycle at a different place. The aim was for each group to identify some points they would like to share with readers who might be in a similar situation. We characterized these points as solidarities (things that bound the group together) and tensions (things they needed to hold rather than resolve in their work and in their relationships). Again these learning points are shared in the three clusters of professional–client relationships, organizations and communities.

A criticism of what follows is that the biblical themes have had an implicit rather than explicit impact on this final stage of the discussion. Chapter 5 conveyed some of the difficulties that arose in turning to scripture. As authors we have marked where we feel the biblical themes (A, B and C) can be seen in the conversation, but we are not claiming that the challenges of interpretation raised in Chapter 5 were resolved at the event.

Solidarities and tensions in professional–client relationships

Solidarities

The group agreed two themes to be fundamental to the effectiveness of professional work. The first of these was our relationship with God and the implications of this for our relationships with clients and colleagues.

Relationships

The group identified the quality and nature of the relationships they established with clients and colleagues as fundamental to the effectiveness of their work and to how they lived out their Christian faith in the world and at work. The primary relationship from which the quality of all other relationships flow was seen as the relationship with God: this is the foundation of how we see the world, our being and identity, our thinking, relating, moral life and action.

It was recognized that our personal relationship with God is not a private, individual matter mediated only through our own unique spiritual life and practice; our relationship with God is also mediated through our relationships with others and through the community in which we live and work. In fact, it may often be the case, as in the encounters described above, that it is mediated through our relationships with people who are seen as distinctly other or different from us (Theme B). When we are open to meet with others in their humanity, we are open to encounter both ourselves and God in new and often surprising ways. However, it was also recognized that in order for this primary relationship to deepen and to grow, we need time to be with God and to be with ourselves. It is out of this *being* in God that our *doing* should flow. Practitioners recognized the capacity for being – being comfortable enough to be oneself and simply to be with others without feeling compelled to do anything – and for being present to others (presence) as a quality of relating that promotes healing beyond 'professional competence'. At times of stress and difficulty in our lives, all of us know the healing and strengthening power of having someone that we can go to who is able to 'be there' for us and to give us their undivided attention even though they may not be able to do anything directly to change the current circumstances: it is the quality of their presence that can renew our strength and affirm our own being. For Christian people, the source of our 'being' and the motivation for our 'being there' for others was understood by the group as our relationship with God.

For the professionals in the encounters described above, this understanding of the place and importance of relationship in every aspect of life related to a commitment to reflecting God's covenant of love with us by seeking to work out of 'covenant' as distinct from 'contract' love for others. The practitioners saw the approach to the people they work with as person-centred, in the sense of valuing each person as unique and created in the image of God, rather than instrumental because of the way they see the world as a consequence of their own direct experience of and relationship with God.

As mentioned in Chapter 4, the group moved from positing theological understandings to relationship with God as the foundation for life and work representing a shift from the doctrinal to the experiential as the category with ultimate authority for their lives. Several people in the group spoke of powerful experiences of the presence and reality of God breaking into their lives in unexpected ways and at times when they were least prepared. This grace of God's presence bestowed an experience of transcendence and resulted in the transformation of people's lives. This transcendent dimension to the relationship with God was understood as existing alongside the immanent dimension where God is found in the created order and in our human relationships (Theme A).

Authenticity

Allied to the recognition of the importance of relationship was the recognition of the need for our encounters to be *genuine* human encounters. If we are to bear witness in the world to the faith that animates us, we need to live our lives with authenticity. The group identified that at the heart of effective professional work there needs to be an authenticity that brings belief and action into harmony. In psychotherapeutic terms, there needs to be 'congruence' between what we say and what we do, between what we think and what we feel, between the head and the heart. If we undertake work or work in a way that is at odds with our values and beliefs, then our relationships will not be genuine and our relationship with our self will be conflicted. If, by contrast, we are rooted and grounded in an authentic relationship with God and with ourselves, then we will be secure enough to respond appropriately to the complex personal and organizational situations in which we have to work.

Authenticity therefore can be said to have an ethical and sometimes even a prophetic dimension. If we are authentically grounded in our work and personhood, we will be able to take risks, to challenge appropriately and at times to be 'prophetic' in our words or actions. One practitioner related how their working context became so pressured that they no longer felt that they could give to individuals the attention and care that was required. As a result of this pressure, they perceived that the working practices that the context now demanded involved an increasing level of risk both for clients and for practitioners. In order to remain effective in their role and to continue to practise with authenticity, the practitioner felt that they needed to challenge this situation. As a first response, they sought to effect change within the organization in order to remedy the situation. When the organization failed to listen to requests for change in working practices, the practitioner felt that they needed to act in accordance with their personal and professional beliefs and values and to leave their role (Theme C).

The group recognized that it is not easy to live and work authentically and that to do so may demand of us real sacrifices that have practical consequences for our lives. In this respect, Jesus was identified as the 'benchmark' for how we might live authentic lives: that is, lives lived at one with God and thereby at one with ourselves in our relationships with others.

The question of authenticity was particularly relevant for individuals in relation to the various institutions and organizations with which our lives are bound up. As in the example above, people recognized that it is often very hard to remain our authentic personal and professional selves within a collective context that demands recognition of its own values, beliefs and practices. Individuals may need to work out carefully how much they can accommodate and adapt to the values and ethos of an organization and still remain authentic and true to their own values and way of being. This was seen by the group as a highly significant issue that many people have to face. The question people asked themselves was: do the structures within which we live and work enable us to be our authentic selves or do they prevent us from being so? This question was seen as relating as much to the Church as to other contexts for life and work. Indeed in the church context, where values and beliefs are central to its reason for being, when conflict of this nature does occur, it is often particularly acute and painful to address.

Tensions

The risk of loving commitment in a risk-averse culture

The above consideration of the relationship between structures and the capacity to live an authentic life leads into a consideration of the first of the two main tensions that the group identified as present within their work and relationships: the need to take the risk of loving relationship in a risk-averse culture.

All the practitioners involved in the above encounters were sharply aware of inhabiting an increasingly risk-averse culture. While they were well aware of the need for appropriate professional boundaries and procedures to ensure good practice and the safety of both clients and professionals, they were also aware of substantial organizational pressures stemming from an unrealistic desire to eradicate all risk or at least to reduce it to a bare minimum. This cultural trend was seen as a creeping response to the threat of litigation and to recent financial constraints that have impacted on working practices. For example, within health care, professionals and people working to promote health and wellbeing were seen in the group as being under increased pressure to work with people within tight boundaries and within particular contractual limits. The establishment of evidence-based practice has brought significant benefits to patient care but it has also brought the need for the involvement of professionals to be based on clinical evidence and to bear the expectation of a measurable clinical outcome. This is the basis of the contract that is made with the patient or client. Members of the group pointed out that this risk-averse, contractual and outcome-orientated culture leaves out of the picture the significance of the nature of the human encounter and the many dimensions of health, healing and wellbeing that are not measurable in terms of outcome but may arguably be equally important, not only to the wellbeing of the client, but also to that of the practitioner, the organization and indeed, to our society as a whole. In contrast to an ethos of working strictly within particular contractual limits, discussion in the group described a holistic model of working. This model was seen as stemming from the values and beliefs of the practitioner: the holding of a genuine loving concern for the other that may require the practitioner to take calculated risks and to transgress boundaries in order to facilitate healing (Theme B).

The importance of the themes discussed previously to the holding of this tension is self-evident: the capacity to live with not knowing and the quality and authenticity of relationship are relevant examples. It is this tension that the group characterized in terms of the difference between 'covenant' love, on the analogy of God's covenant with Israel, and 'contract' love. While it could be argued that this is too simplistic a contrast to draw, nevertheless, it does bear witness to a certain truth: it is clear that the practitioners involved in the discussion felt the tension that it sought to describe.

In the three encounters described above, it is certainly the case that practitioners took the risk of moving beyond strict contractual boundaries. David continued to be there for Darren even though it was no longer possible to predict what particular outcomes might be; Pat continued to support Jean in caring for the children, even though she did not know where it might lead; Tom was willing to negotiate the boundaries of his contract as a religious professional in order to respect the integrity of Mark's life. In each of these encounters, when the practitioners had come to the end of their strictly demarcated 'professional' helping repertoire, they chose not to abandon but to remain committed to the person in need of their help and support and in so doing embraced the risk of loving commitment.

Professional identity and Christian identity

The second main tension that the group identified was that between the role that they inhabited at work and their self-identity as a Christian person. In discussion, the example was given of a manager who had to make a hard decision about the suitability of an employee for their role while, at the same time, the manager understood their difficult personal circumstances, recognized their needs and wanted to offer the person pastoral support. This kind of role conflict had to be managed with integrity and it was recognized that the way in which such situations are negotiated may be as important as the outcomes for people's wellbeing.

It is this same tension between the professional and Christian identity that Tom had to hold in his encounter with Mark. As a religious 'professional' he might have provided a straightforward, 'orthodox' Christian funeral liturgy for the family. However, Tom knew that this would be inappropriate in the circumstances and would risk failing to connect with the mourners. Instead, drawing on his own Christian understanding and identity, he negotiated the boundaries around the service and in so doing, was able to hold successfully the tension he felt in the service of those he was seeking to help.

This tension was identified by the group as having a wider cultural context. Members who worked in a secular environment identified a widespread phenomenon: people applaud and encourage those who work with integrity and have a genuine commitment to the work, but if that person's relationship with work arises from the Christian values and beliefs that they espouse, the organization tries not to allow any explicit allusion to the Christian values that underpin the way of working. People in the group identified this as a pressure from secular contexts to prise apart the congruence of word and deed. Secular agencies might well welcome a certain kind of dedicated engagement and action but they stop short of being willing to acknowledge any reference it may have to a basis in faith. When people encountered this cultural fissure, it was seen as encountering a boundary that has the potential to exclude important aspects of self-identity which can make it difficult for people to be authentic at work. Once again it was felt that organizational culture and structures have the power to constrain people and to set the agenda for how work is undertaken. If practitioners are to be authentic and to find a fruitful integration of their professional and Christian identities, it was recognized as being important to take time to reflect on their work in a given context in order to identify the tensions and pressures that do exist and so to be able to explore ways of negotiating the tensions that they meet as a person of faith. Group members were left with the question: Who ultimately sets the agenda and what power, control or influence might Christian practitioners have over the kind of agenda that is set and the way in which it is carried out? (Theme C).

The group ended its reflection by acknowledging that there is a fundamental tension inherent in seeking to live out a Christian life in the world and that the way in which Christian people negotiate and hold these tensions in lives of authentic Christian witness is crucial for the health and wellbeing of both clients and practitioners and for the effectiveness and integrity of their professional relationships.

Solidarities and tensions in organizations

As with the other sections articulating this part of the process, the material will be divided into two, points of solidarity and points of tension. It was clear by the end of the discussion presented in Chapter 4 that the subject of human flourishing had become an overriding concern – to what extent could the practices encountered in both secular and religious worlds be deemed life-enhancing or life-denying? How do they contribute to or inhibit the search for human wellbeing? From discussions in the wider group at the conference other common themes had started to emerge also, particularly that of risk, and the apparent fact that it was when people or organizations were prepared to step outside their normal comfort zones and to take chances, that the more creative work and improved relationships were likely to develop. This is not the same as the constant processes of change which seem pervasive in the public and commercial sectors and which tend to meet resistance in the faith domain. Change, in itself, is not to be equated with risk. Sometimes the riskier course of action is to do nothing and to leave things as they are, or else to work against the grain of proposed changes. In terms of the organizational world, we attempted to explore further examples of where we believed churches could identify with and learn from good practice in the secular environment, but in the religious context we found ourselves encountering zones of frustration with the way that churches often operate and their unwillingness or incapacity to respond to positive opportunities across the divide.

Solidarities

Practices that are life-enhancing

The first point of solidarity comes from the experience of a member of the small group who had been a board member of a Housing Association for 14 years, but in his capacity as a parish priest concerned for issues of affordable housing rather than with any specific business expertise. During that time he became involved in the Equality and Diversity agenda of the Association which was, of course, being driven down through many organizations by a wider government agenda. There have been many areas where those of faith have been rightly wary of or questioning of the general 'political correctness movement' under the Labour regime, but this was encountered as a positive movement where one could identify with the core values of what was being proposed.

What was so impressive about the process introduced by this particular Housing Association was the actual training for both board members and staff that was put into place. Without going into the details of this, the trainer employed was not only an impressive adult educator, but had the ability to get to the heart of all types of discriminatory behaviour and attitudes. His technique was to take ordinary situations where one might not even think one was acting or thinking in a discriminatory fashion, and to show how this was in fact the case. All participants found themselves challenged to look at themselves and ask some searching questions. This was not done in a way that set out to make people feel guilty, but more as a raising of self-awareness with a view to working for greater justice.

The impact upon this particular board member, who had taken on the role in the organization of Equality and Diversity Champion, and was therefore responsible with certain senior officers for tracking this process through the board and staff, was profound. The values being communicated were ones that he felt a person of faith should sign up to and support. The way that the training was conducted was itself an eye-opener and an object lesson in adult education in its own right. Having been heavily involved in adult education in church circles, the individual concerned had an appreciation of what was being done and recognized that most church-based equivalents were inferior to this. Then the success of the training in helping people turn the spotlight on themselves and to really examine their own attitudes and behaviour had something akin to the power of a conversion experience in religious terms, but done in a subtle and enabling manner rather than through browbeating or guilt trips.

It felt as though a model developed and delivered from within the organizational world had much to commend it and could offer insights into personal development that would be of value in a religious setting. So the general objective was indeed that of furthering human flourishing and enhancing levels of wellbeing as shared by all as the Blurred Encounters conference progressed. The positive message was that people's attitudes and understandings could indeed be changed and that this was not simply a piece of management 'window dressing' going through the motions of a movement that was being enforced by an external political agenda. It required the trainer to take risks with himself and being completely open about his own colour and sexuality – that is being black and gay. In other words, it was a classic blurred encounter where deeply held beliefs were communicated powerfully and effectively but from within a wholly secular context. Hence this is offered as a point of solidarity between the two worlds and where someone of faith could recognize what was being communicated as 'kingdom values' (Theme B).

The common use of personal development

The second instance of solidarity is related to the first in that it involves attempts to increase self-awareness. One of the group is a team leader within a research establishment and therefore responsible for both the work and welfare of the team members. As a person of faith he has a concern for the whole person, not simply how they function in a narrow or mechanical fashion. He shares with the group as a whole, the conviction that if human beings are respected and shown the consideration they deserve, then they are more likely to perform well in their work. Achieving this, however, is not straightforward within a highly pressured working environment where targets and objectives dominate the scene. In discussion with another member of the group who is now a consultant, the general subject of approaches to increased self-awareness within organizations was explored more fully.

A wide variety of such techniques is now available to and familiar within the business world. Among these is the use of Myers-Briggs (derived from a Jungian base), the Enneagram, the Belbin self-perception inventory, and what has become known as the Spirituality at Work movement. All of us had experienced at least some of these, either in the workplace or through their employment in a faith context. Myers-Briggs and the Enneagram are well established in certain church circles as aids to identifying one's preferred prayer life for instance. While it is both right and natural to express a degree of scepticism, both about the approaches themselves, and also about the ways in which they are sometime employed, it was felt that they are attempting to give attention to the human and thus to be taken seriously. It would be easy to dismiss them as no more accurate or convincing than horoscopes when it comes to understanding or predicting one's own behaviour, but the experience of those of us at the conference was that they did indeed have some value when it comes to deepening our own self-understanding.

It is also clear that this is not simply about the individual, but also helps in working out how individuals operate in teams and in relationships with others. Belbin, for instance, is very much about discovering the particular roles that people play within a team, acknowledging that these will not necessarily remain constant but will vary according to context. It was felt that since much church life is now also team based, whether we talk about clergy teams, or clergy–laity mixed, or also now ministry teams consisting of laity only, to have access to something like Belbin could be extremely illuminating and valuable. Tensions between people and the power struggles that often develop could perhaps be better understood and contained if such techniques were employed in a church setting. So this might meet two objectives. That of helping individuals gain a better self-understanding and greater self-awareness, both of which are part of personal and spiritual development, and that of how to cooperate more effectively with others in the shared tasks of ministry.

There were also reservations expressed, however, particularly over organizational motivations for using these techniques. Some in the group had first-hand experience of meditation techniques and broad-based spirituality, which was not deeply embedded in any one particular tradition, being used by organizations to help people cope with stress at work. While this is not illegitimate in itself, it raised deeper questions of what might be wrong in the organization that such stress levels were so prevalent. In other words, treating symptoms rather than causes might not be consistent with a real concern for human wellbeing, and might be a 'papering over of the cracks' rather than addressing underlying issues that a more prophetic approach would bring to the surface. So the techniques might be a means to an end for the organization, that of keeping people 'happy', or at least 'happy enough' not to rock the boat or ask difficult questions. Cases would need to be considered individually to decide what was really happening, with the acknowledgement that it is often difficult to reach unambiguous conclusions.

Are religious groups always immune from the temptation to employ self-awareness techniques in a more cynical and instrumental manner? It was thought not, and assessment procedures for potential ordinands and other leaders were mentioned in this regard. The introduction of Common

Tenure in the Church of England, and the attached require-ments for appraisal or ministry review, are seen by some as being mechanical and potentially oppressive. There is a ten-dency to adopt what are 'good ideas' from the secular world, either without a full understanding of how they work, or without the resources to implement them properly. So there are dangers as well as possible advantages. But we could cer-tainly see points of solidarity and common ground in this area of personal and group development.

Tensions

A failure of pastoral care

A point of tension identified by the group arose from an ac-count that has not yet been described, so a brief explanation is required. This particular group member is a head teacher from a Church of England primary school in an urban set-ting. Up until recently, with an established incumbent in post, there had been regular and consistent contact between the parish priest and the school, through assemblies, services in church, membership of the governing body, and the sort of pastoral relationships that can only be built up over a long period of time. This particular minister has now retired, and the diocesan authorities have not appointed a replacement for him. The head has been appealing to local church lead-ers to provide the regular contact that existed until a few months ago, but the result of this is that the various tasks are being covered by different clergy, each trying to do their best, but unable to fulfil the whole role as it existed before. Hence what is being lost is consistent pastoral contact with the school, both staff and children. In other words, a prime opportunity for relationship is going begging, and the mis-sion of the Church to reach out to young families in the area is being severely hampered. Attempts by the head to get this recognized and responded to seem to be falling on deaf ears as the Church struggles to re-organize itself and work out a strategy for the future.

So there is frustration within the school with the Church as an institution as it seems unable to cope with obvious pastoral opportunities while it decides how to proceed in terms of staffing and deployment. The gap between how one profession deals with vacancies (the teaching profession) and how the Church operates, almost suggests to the committed but unsupported staff that the Church is not capable of behaving in a professional manner. Not only is an opportunity being missed therefore, but the message being given by the religious authorities is that they are not operating effectively as an organization. It is not clear what can be done about this particular problem in the short term, but it does raise the wider issue of what sort of an organization the Church actually is, and whether it might not benefit from being better structured and organized.

It is not as simple as saying that churches are voluntary organizations, because they do have a number of full-time and part-time staff, and how they are deployed is critical to how well the volunteers can then operate. Perhaps good outcomes do depend upon good organization and it will not do for the Church to claim immunity from criticism on the grounds that it has little or no control over how its staff operate. Once one has had experience of good practice in secular organizations, the churches can appear amateurish and even incompetent. Can this be addressed, and, if so, how? If the Church is to be taken seriously in the professional public and business environment, it must learn to function in a more transparent and efficient way. This is a considerable challenge for those who find themselves crossing the boundaries and trying to earn credibility for faith groups in the organizational world.

Implementing pastoral care

The second tension returns to the recurrent theme of change and is clearly related to the example just narrated. It is how change is implemented that is critical to this discussion, and the extent to which a humane approach is adopted. As has been noted, faith groups who set great store by tradition and the authority of a specific text, often find it difficult to justify change at all. One argument against it is that the religious groups feel they are bowing to or giving way to the fashions of the age, rather than showing adherence to their tradition. The burden of proof must therefore be upon those arguing for change, who have to do so in terms of the accepted authority irrespective of the merits of the case. In secular organizations the burden of proof is more likely to be the other way round. If it is clear that the proposed changes are going to be of bene-fit, then those who oppose cannot simply appeal to the past, but must shape their arguments in terms of those benefits and show that they are not as important as is being supposed. This makes understanding, let alone agreement between the two worlds very difficult to achieve, as they are operating with different assumptions about how to proceed.

But that is only part of the problem as the issue of how change is being put into practice often throws the limelight on secular organizations that may place achieving the objective above the personal considerations of those involved. Changes are sometime 'steamrollered through' or imposed from above without adequate warning or consultation, leaving those at the sharp end demoralized and confused. In so much of the public sector, for instance, people are not given enough time to absorb or embed one set of changes before another lot is then brought in. Quality of service then suffers and morale and job satisfaction sink further. This means that the mod-els of change management practised in secular organizations can themselves leave a lot to be desired and are open to the criticism that they fail to take the human beings involved into account. Hence it is not straightforward to argue that the churches have got the process of change wrong while secular organizations have got it right. There are problems and inadequacies on both sides of the boundary.

Perhaps the question that needs to be raised is that of the objectives of the specific changes being proposed and of what principles, if any, lie behind them. Change for the sake of change appears arbitrary and futile, but equally holding on to the past just because it is the past seems no better. Under what circumstances can change be justified and how must it be implemented if it is to be brought about humanely? The lack of awareness of the differences and the general failure to address these questions by both sides in the discussion is a real barrier to cooperation and understanding. Therefore we conclude that it constitutes another point of tension between religious and secular as they encounter one another.

Solidarities and tensions in communities

Solidarity: a desire for regeneration to be humanizing but the need to mobilize bridging and linking social capital to make this happen

Marginalized communities need resources from outside their boundaries to assist with the task of regeneration. However, those external resources often wish to dictate terms, most usually to satisfy the requirements of government policy that arise from a local or national political mandate. Where those policies do not mesh with the reality of the life of the community there is a real danger that they are dehumanizing in their effect and do not lead to human flourishing. An example would be the drive to improve the standard of education delivered in all schools. The setting of targets for pupil attainment and then putting schools into league tables has served in marginalized communities to stigmatize yet further the schools that serve them. However, the market is also an actor and so for example the withdrawal of branches of financial services organizations from a community can leave room for loan sharks charging punishing rates of interest.

If Christian practitioners are to play a role in humanizing external initiatives they need to help the community build its own social capital as a basis from which to argue its case for a contextualized response. Examples of bridging social capital would include tenants associations, community centres, children's centres and churches and other faith institutions. These groups create bridging social capital by bringing together residents of different backgrounds with a shared interest. They provide a point of contact for service-providing agencies to consult with people with an interest in the community. However, the reality of local politics is that groups with connections outside the local community are likely to be more powerful. This is because they can access information about what is happening to other communities, build networks that can touch influential people and bring their issues to the attention of local and national government. This all-important linking social capital is often developed by 'those in the know', that is those with links outside the locality. Churches often have an important role to play with their local, countywide, regional, national and global networks.

Christian practitioners can often play a vital role of communication. For those working for government or voluntary agencies they can adopt a commitment to ensure that information about proposals is communicated in a language that residents can understand and in a number of formats that will be accessible to them. Ministers can often find themselves acting as interpreters between official language and the reality of the community. Effective communication lies at the heart of bridging and linking. Where it is feared that proposals will be dehumanizing, ministers can often help residents speak out and Christian practitioners can adopt a willingness to listen and to promote the face-to-face contact that residents often want.

During the discussion of the different contexts in which we worked, we identified the need for bridging and linking between four different players to increase the effectiveness of community regeneration. First, the outsider who, while seen as a regeneration expert, could also legitimately claim first-hand knowledge of marginalized communities. Second, the insider with a desire to make connections beyond the boundaries of the community. A locally resident priest or minister could often take that role. Third, a core group of local people who were willing to buy into the regeneration process and be active in it. Fourth, a wider group of community members who felt that they were genuinely being informed and involved rather than consulted in a way that induced cynicism and a feeling of being 'done to'. The interconnection between these four actors could act as a humanizing force on regeneration and other community development initiatives. This solidarity drew upon the boundary-crossing love exemplified in the ministry of Jesus (Theme B).

Solidarity: spiritual regeneration seen as releasing the capacity for reflection so that outer and inner worlds are in conversation

Arguing for a spiritual dimension to community regeneration can be difficult when working with agencies that take a secularist or 'faith-blind' perspective. However, a common criticism of residents of marginalized communities is that they are passive about their situation and over-dependent upon the state for their day-to-day income and needs. This suggests a lack of agency or power over their own lives. The Christian tradition sees human agency as being strengthened by God's grace. This suggests a connection between the inner world of the human spirit and the outer world of the community in which they live. What activities might enable a community to reconnect with the capacity for reflection and so strengthen their capacity to act? For the Christian community, prayer and worship would be important means of grace. However, we also had examples of the arts being used to activate a sense of inner well being that developed a capacity to act. The example of the community choir in Chapter 4 shows how bringing a group of people to support each other in an activity that required listening, reflective capacity and team work increased their confidence in other areas of their life. A further example would be the use of hospitality in the winter night shelter to enable homeless people to feel like guests, valued for who they were, rather than as a problem to be solved. The experience of hospitality, eating together and serving one another was transformative for guests and hosts. For guests it gave them a sense of being more than a cog in the system and for the hosts it gave them a sense that by simple actions they could make a difference to a persistent social problem in their neighbourhood. To advocate for the spiritual regeneration of communities was to seek the coming of the kingdom on earth. The aim was to enable residents to be fully human rather than the objects of policy (Theme A).

Tension: dealing with conflicting pressures to respond to community needs and individual needs

Christian practitioners in agencies serving deprived communities can feel bound by their role to engage either with structural issues or with individuals they are employed to work with. Breaking free of those role constraints was difficult but with determination it was possible to have sufficient contact with individuals to give a perspective on structural change or sufficient contact with structures to advocate on behalf of individuals. For ministers and priests resident in the community the pressures were much greater because they had roles with unclear boundaries. There could be expectations from church attenders that their role was to provide worship and pastoral care for them. There could be expectations from the wider church and other agencies that they were there primarily to engage in community development. Just as heroic leadership has been identified as a way of dealing with schools in the form of 'super-heads' who can deal with individual and structural problems, there was a danger of seeking 'super-vicars' who can span the boundaries of individual and community concerns. The ways of avoiding this 'saviour syndrome' were not simple. Helping church members locate Christ in each other rather than just in a priest so as to extend the capacity for pastoral care was one route but a challenging one in a context where dependency was a dominant way of living. Helping priests and ministers locate and make use of appropriate support was another important safeguard. People under stress tend to disconnect from the sources of support available to them. Churches under stress can often disconnect from wider church structures and the support they might offer.

In the end there is no easy solution to the dilemma of individual versus community. Those with unclear role descriptions will need to make choices. Skills in reading and interpreting daily encounters and reflecting upon them can facilitate seeing the community need in the individual case and the impact on individuals of structural decisions.

Tension: understanding poverty as a sub-culture to be eliminated versus a counter-culture to be valued

Poverty can be viewed as injustice, as a state where a group of people have insufficient resources for human flourishing at the same time as others in their society have more than sufficient. Poverty can cause material, emotional and social deprivation with opportunities that are curtailed or not taken up. We know that poverty correlates with other sorts of deprivation such as poor health and low educational achievement. Given this perspective it seems obvious that Christians should be active in eliminating poverty whether through working with individuals, organizations or communities.

However, there is another strand of Christian thought that views poverty as a state of simplicity and therefore happiness. An ability to become detached from material and social goods prized by a wider society and yet find a way of living in relationship with family and friends without these trophies. In a deeply materialistic society, where even children are treated instrumentally for what they can achieve, it is valuable to have people witnessing to the possibility of living aside from instrumental goals.

Recent debates about inequality suggest that the experience of poverty is more distressing when the person is aware of the material goods and opportunities experienced by others in proximity to them. The growing class of super-rich have made even those with more than adequate incomes feel discontent and ill at ease. This would suggest that poverty is a mental as well as a material condition. This tension is present in the beatitudes that Matthew's Gospel renders as 'poor in spirit' and Luke's as 'poor'.

The context setting material at the end of the Introduction showed how the Coalition Government is seeking to develop its own understanding of poverty. Ideas about wellbeing are helpfully being added to the lexicon of poverty. However, the dependency of the super-rich on their possessions is not identified and the voices of those advocating a less materialistic lifestyle, although present at the margins, are rarely amplified.

Concluding commentary

This chapter has sought to record the practical wisdom that participants at the event wished to pass on. It brings to a close the pastoral cycle and the authors' attempt to convey on paper the experience of the action learning event. The solidarities and tensions identified can be seen as a tentative attempt at public theology. They are both an attempt to take part in public debates using Christian reasoning and also to think theologically about issues of public, social and economic policy. However, they do not offer a public theology 'from above' about how professional–client relations, organizational life and community regeneration should be undertaken. Rather, they offer 'from below' the results of a conversation about how Christian practice might be a more faithful witness to the kingdom of heaven. We look forward to readers' evaluations of this attempt to bridge pastoral practice and public theology. The final chapter tries to offer our reflections on what we have learned from engaging in this process.

Conclusion:

Anticipating Further Encounters

Practical theology works in ways that are provisional. Each cycle of action and reflection brings participants to a new place but that place is one which raises further questions for reflection. This book has sought to give voice to a particular conversation but it also seeks to open up that conversation to further participants. A key task for the Church is discerning God's mission in the world, and we believe that many of the points made in this book can contribute to that discernment. Those who work at the interface of church and world need to be in constant communication so that the signs of the times can be read and a faithful response made.

This chapter returns to the purposes of the book set out in the Introduction and evaluates what contribution has been made. The first purpose was to provide an example of a process of theological reflection and so the rewards and challenges of theological reflection are assessed in the first section of the chapter. The second purpose was to bring into conversation two groups in the Church who have a shared concern about the impact of institutional structures on individuals. The second section of the chapter looks at how further conversations might be brought about. The chapter finishes with some reflections from the authors on the theme of Human Flourishing which try to summarize where their thinking has got to as a result of writing the book.

The rewards and challenges of theological reflection

The first purpose of the book was to provide an example of a process of theological reflection with a commentary on the practical problems encountered. Three challenges in using theological reflection have been discovered. The first is the need to find a trigger for the conversation if participants do not share the same context. In the case of the event described in this book, the concept of 'blurred encounters' was something potential participants were able to identify with and recognize sufficiently to respond to with examples of their own. The second challenge is to assess whether participants have sufficiently shared skills in interpreting the Christian tradition to navigate that part of the process successfully. While not wanting to dismiss the valuable outcomes that have come from the event, this issue could be viewed as a derailment. Christopher Rowland's exploration of it in Chapter 5 offers some valuable pointers as to further work that needs to be done in building capacity for theological reflection. The third challenge is to ask if the model of the pastoral cycle has been stretched too far beyond its normal purposes. Is it a suitable framework for a conversation that brings people together with the intention of discovering if they have a common agenda that can be theologically understood. It is more normally understood to be about transforming practice or communities and the lack of an on-going life for the group of participants may have subverted the model.

Three rewards have been identified. The first is the value of reflecting theologically in groups without a shared context but with a shared interest. There is a danger in writing a book about an experiential process that readers will say, 'I've read about it, so I don't need to try it.' Theological reflection is a practice that needs practice. Like any skill worth having, each performance generates learning for the next occasion and increases confidence that setbacks can be overcome. The book has been produced out of a conviction that there are important discussions in the Church that are not happening. Those in church-based ministry who have institutional encounters and those working in institutions as chaplains, professionals or managers who have pastoral encounters have much to say to each other but rarely the opportunity to say it. With some networking it should be possible to identify some conversation partners and a facilitator who will help get the first conversation going. Even meeting just four times a year can be sufficient to support the habit of theological reflection and to move it beyond thoughtful ruminating about the pressures of the day.

Like all action learning, theological reflection is a creative process whose outcome cannot be predicted at the outset. For those used to working in agenda-driven settings, the open-ended nature of theological reflection can raise the fear that it will be unproductive. For those working in situations that are resistant to change it can be difficult to believe that something as mundane as a conversation with colleagues can be potentially transformative. The emotional self-awareness that is developed in training for the ministry and professional practice can be harnessed to sit with the chaos of blurred encounters and wait for them to yield their learning, so the second reward is knowing that reflecting with others is helpful in sustaining the patience that the wrestling will yield a blessing.

The final reward of theological reflection that this section proposes is the way it develops our capacity to cross boundaries. The question 'Who is my neighbour?' raised in Chapter 2, remains one of the most profound in the gospel. As a Christian minister or practitioner to whom do I owe a duty of care and what form should that care take at this time in this place? Are there people I habitually regard as strangers who in fact need to be recognized at neighbours? How can I cross boundaries in emulation of Christ's love rather than calculate risk and reward? This is not to advocate foolish practice or a crossing of professional boundaries that damages our neighbour but to remain ever aware of where the boundaries are set and open to the possibility they might be blurred. As has already been suggested, these are decisions best taken in company rather than alone. They are not a matter of 'taking advice' but being open to the creativity of conversation that takes place with the Christian tradition drawn into the discussion.

Two groups in conversation: rules of engagement

The second purpose of the book was to bring into conversation two groups in the Church who have a shared concern about the impact of institutional structures on individuals. The first group were church-based ministers who in addition to their pastoral work took on extra responsibilities that brought them into contact with institutional pressures in secular organizations. The second group were chaplains and lay Christians working in secular institutions but reflecting upon the pastoral encounters they had in their work. Standing back from the conversations summarized in this book we would want to propose some rules of engagement for further conversations.

Given that a key argument of this book is that we need to be willing to accept challenges to cherished beliefs and practices, it may seem odd that the first rule of engagement is to propose that the reflector must know where they are coming from. This is not to recommend a rigid or static position. It is to recommend a reflexivity about one's own position and context that gives a secure position from which change can take place. If knowledge of my own position is limited or uninformed by feedback from others, challenges to my position are likely to seem threatening. I can only be open to the opportunity of blurring boundaries if I know where those boundaries lie and the beliefs and values that inform them. If I am fearful of being swallowed alive by my present context, I cannot be 'eaten well' and digest the new possibilities that may come from an honest encounter with someone who at first inspection I see as 'different' or 'other'. If I am to have the confidence to name and unmask the powers, I need a knowledge of my context that gets below the surface and does not shy away from the political. I need to read both pastoral and institutional encounters, knowing that each will inform the other. It is a key conclusion of this book that disciplined regular theological reflection can develop self-knowledge, enhance skill in reading encounters and facilitate discernment.

Sustaining authenticity and faithfulness is the second rule of engagement. Being a Christian practitioner is to constantly seek after congruence between head, heart and hand. The disruption to that congruence which blurred encounters can create is to be welcomed rather than feared. If the aim of ministry and practice is faithfulness rather than success, challenges to authenticity can be worked through and benefited from. Sustaining authenticity does not happen by wishing it to be so. It requires a number of intentional practices that have been honed over the years. Among them are likely to be adequate time away from work, adequate time for prayer and personal reflection, one-to-one support including such things as spiritual direction, work consultancy or supervision, and opportunities to learn and reflect in the company of others. This book has voiced the honest reflections of practitioners working with marginalized communities and client groups. It is easy, in identifying with that marginalization, to become cut off from needed sources of support and from the wider life of the Church. Authenticity can sometimes be glimpsed in the mirror but it more usually depends upon trusted sources of feedback who will tell us plainly when we are 'not ourselves' and encourage us to reflect. Sometimes our understanding of faithful practice can be warped by a world that works to squeeze us into its mould. Building our own empire can at times seem more attractive than working for the coming of the kingdom. Subjecting our goals to scrutiny and discernment from trusted others helps in setting priorities and saves us from becoming indispensable.

Knowing where I am coming from and being active in sustaining authenticity and faithfulness may seem unglamorous rules of engagement but they are essential if the messiness of reality is to be met rather than avoided.

So what is human flourishing?

This book has tried to show that pastoral practice and public theology belong to each other and can refresh each other in the search for human flourishing. We hope that readers will not be able to separate the two in the chapters that describe the action learning event.

This book has attempted to listen in to conversations seeking human flourishing. It has suggested that it is worth seeking a common view of what this entails as a guide to shared action. It has acknowledged that there are agendas that often shape the work of Christian ministers and practitioners that focus on bare survival rather than life in all its fullness.

The authors have had the privilege of re-reading and discussing the material generated by the action learning event. We cannot speak for all the situations mentioned in this book, but in conclusion we want to offer three factors which seem to us to be significant.

Giving up the illusion of control – receiving humility

So many of the issues wrestled with in this book have been about the temptation to succeed by exercising more control:

the next piece of evidence-based practice that will make things 'right' for the client; the next reorganization that will make the organization perform better; the next regeneration project that will turn this into a desirable place to live. Humility before the complexity of the human condition and belief that the chaos can lead to creativity seem approaches more likely to lead to flourishing.

> Yes, my condition is a very challenging one to live with, but it is not different from yours. What I am grappling with is not Multiple Sclerosis, it is the human condition. I don't know what the future holds – but neither do you. I don't know what is essentially me, but neither do you. I am not in control of my body, but neither are you. The difference now I have MS, is that it is less easy than it was to delude myself otherwise. This is a new exciting country, and I am exploring it right where I am. (Ind, 2000)

It is not that we are called to be passive, far from it. It is that we are co-creators with God. We must not exaggerate our impact any more than we must hide from our talents. We work for the coming of the kingdom, we enjoy its fruits but we accept that its final fulfilment lies outside our hands. We remain ready to risk losing our life in order to gain it.

Engaging in dialogue to maintain a sense of reality and to gain energy – receiving grace

As this chapter has already emphasized, a key temptation for Christian ministers and practitioners under pressure is to go it alone. In supporting people through work consultancy, a common pair of questions is to ask: What gives you energy? What drains energy? People vary as to the level of contact with others they find energizing or draining but it is rare to find someone who does not find conversation with trusted partners about matters of shared concern to be a means of grace. Most often people note with sadness the infrequency of such discussions and the amount of 'surface conversations' that disappoint. There can be a false sense of self-sufficiency that as an experienced practitioner such dialogue should be left behind or a sense that giving advice to more junior colleagues is the measure of seniority. Taking the step of engaging in dialogue is often to discover with a sense of relief that others too hunger and thirst after righteousness and so want to retain a sense of reality.

Finding a balance between structure and agency – receiving freedom

A final temptation is to feel that we need to choose between structure and agency. By temperament some people require clear structures if they are to contribute effectively, whereas others find structure inhibiting. The metaphor of a string vest contains the mystery of why something so insubstantial holds in the heat. The gaps between the string need to be big enough to hold the warm air but not so big that the heat escapes. To put it more directly, we need enough structure to make things happen but enough freedom to ensure something really happens. Too much structure and creativity is stifled, too little structure and individual efforts dissipate. Finding the right balance in any situation is challenging but once found it can release people to be all they can be.

In conclusion . . .

In this book we have tried to describe and critique a process of theological reflection in the hopes that it will encourage others to embark on their own processes of theological reflection. We took risks in setting up a conversation that we felt wasn't happening elsewhere in the Church. We learned things we did not expect to. We engaged in genuine dialogue that has changed our thinking. We found that in real life, theological reflection is messier than the models imply. But we were left with the promise of theological reflection as right discernment in a world of blurred encounters. Through this theological conversation we can gain the confidence and grace to act as flourishing humans while recognizing that the world is not yet as God desires.

Bibliography

Atherton, J., C. Baker, J. and Reader (2011), *Christianity and the New Social Order*, London: SPCK.

Ballard, P. (2009), 'Locating Chaplaincy: a theological note', *Crucible* 48 (July – September).

Barton, J. (2007), *The Nature of Biblical Criticism*, Louiseville, KY: Westminster John Knox Press.

Bennett, Z. and C. Rowland (2005), 'Contextual and advocacy readings of the Bible', in P. Ballard and S. Holmes (eds), *The Bible in Pastoral Practice: Readings in the Place and Function of Scripture in the Church*, London: Darton, Longman and Todd, pp. 174–90.

Blond, P. (2010), *Red Tory: How Left and Right have Broken Britain and How We Can Fix It*, London: Faber and Faber.

Boff, C. (1987), *Theology and Praxis: Epistemological Foundations*, Maryknoll, NY: Orbis Books.

Bretherton, L. (2010), *Christianity and Contemporary Politics: The Conditions and Possibilities of Faithful Witness*, Oxford: Wiley-Blackwell.

Brueggemann, W. (2005), 'The re-emergence of Scripture: post-liberalism', in P. Ballard and S. Holmes (eds), *The Bible in Pastoral Practice: Readings in the Place and Function of Scripture in the Church*, London: Darton, Longman and Todd, pp. 152–73.

Cameron, H. (2010), *Resourcing Mission: Practical Theology for Changing Churches*, London: SCM Press.

CBCEW (2008), *Choosing the Common Good*, Stoke on Trent: Alive Publishing.

Chaplin, J. (2008), *Talking God: The Legitimacy of Religious Public Reasoning,* London: Theos.

CSAN (2011), *A Common Endeavour, A Call to Deeper Social Engagement Report 1,* London: CSAN.

CSAN (2011), *Catholic Social Teaching and the philosophy behind the 'Big Society', A Call to Deeper Social Engagement Report 2,* London: CSAN.

CSAN (2011). *Building a New Culture of Social Responsibility, A Call to Deeper Social Engagement Report 3,* London, CSAN.

Dean, H. (2010), *Understanding Human Need: Social Issues, Policy and Practice,* Bristol: Policy Press.

Freire, P. (1972), *Pedagogy of the Oppressed,* London: Penguin Book Ltd.

Gadamer, H.-G.(2004), *Truth and Method,* London: Continuum.

Graham, E. (2008), 'Why Practical Theology Must Go Public', *Practical Theology* 1(1), pp. 11–17.

Graham, E., H. Walton, and F. Ward, (2005), *Theological Reflection: Methods,* London: SCM Press.

Green, L. (2002), *Let's Do Theology,* London: Continuum.

H+ Making Good Sense of the Bible (2011) Bible Society Resource– www.hplus.org.uk

Heelas, P., L. Woodhead, *et al.* (2005), *The Spiritual Revolution: Why Religion is Giving Way to Spirituality,* Oxford: Blackwell Publishing.

Heywood, D. (2011), *Reimagining Ministry,* London: SCM Press.

Holland, J. and P. Henriot (1985), *Social Analysis: Linking Faith and Justice,* Maryknoll, NY: Orbis Books.

Ind, J. (2000), 'Finding my Bearings in a Strange Country – Multiple Sclerosis', *Third Way* 23(2).

Kolb, David A. (1983), Experiental Learning: Experience as the Source of Learning and Development. New Jersey, FT Prenctice Hall.

Latour, B. (2004), *Politics of Nature,* Cambridge, MA: Harvard University Press.

Lynch, G. (2005), *Understanding Theology and Popular Culture*, Oxford: Blackwell Publishing.

Nash, S. and P. Nash, (2009), *Tools for Reflective Ministry*, London: SPCK.

Pattison, S. (2008), 'Is pastoral care dead in a mission-led church?', *Practical Theology* 1(1), pp. 7–10.

Reader, J. (1994), *Local Theology: Church and Community in Dialogue*, London: SPCK.

Reader, J. (2005), *Blurred Encounters: A Reasoned Practice of Faith*, Cardiff: Aureus Publishing.

Reader, J. (2008), *Reconstructing Practical Theology: The Impact of Globalization*, Aldershot: Ashgate.

Reader, J. and C. Baker (eds) (2009), *Entering the New Theological Space*, Aldershot: Ashgate.

Schon, Donald A. (1983), The Reflective Practitioner: How Professionals Think in Action. New York, Basic Books.

Shier-Jones, A. (2009), *Pioneer Ministry and Fresh Expressions of Church*, London: SPCK.

Sugirtharajah, R. S. (1991), *Voices from the Margin: Interpreting the Bible in the Third World*, London: SPCK.

Swinton, J. (2009), 'Is Theological Reflection a Technique or a Virtue?; conference paper: www.biapt.org.uk/tr5.shtml.

Thompson, J. and S. Pattison (2005), 'Reflecting on Reflection: Problems and Prospects for Theological Reflection', *Contact* 146, pp. 8–15.

Thompson, J., S. Pattison, and R. Thompson (2008), *SCM Studyguide to Theological Reflection*, London: SCM Press.

Trible, P. (2002), *Texts of Terror: Literary-Feminist Readings of Biblical Narratives*, London: SCM.

Volf, M. (2010), *Captive to the Word of God: Engaging the Scriptures for Contemporary Theological Reflection*, Grand Rapids, MI: William B Eerdmans.

Ward, F. (2005), *Lifelong Learning: Theological Education and Supervision*, London: SCM Press.

Webster, A. (2002), *Wellbeing*, London: SCM Press.

Websites referred to in the Introduction

Centre for Social Justice – www.centreforsocialjustice.org.uk

Ekklesia – www.ekklesia.co.uk

ResPublica Think-tank – respublica.org.uk

Theos – Public Theology Think-Tank – www.theosthinktank.
co.uk

St Paul's Institute – www.stpaulsinstitute.org.uk